KNACK®
MAKE IT EASY

PLANNING YOUR WEDDING

KNACK®

PLANNING YOUR WEDDING

A Step-by-Step Guide to Creating Your Perfect Day

BLAIR deLAUBENFELS, CHRISTY WEBER, AND KIM BAMBERG
CREATORS OF JUNEBUGWEDDINGS.COM

KNACK
MAKE IT EASY

Guilford, Connecticut
An imprint of Globe Pequot Press

can discover ways to uniquely express it. In Chapter 2 we'll show you how to find the right tools to get started, maintain a budget, and stay organized, and we'll give you a step by step schedule so you can make it all happen with plenty of time left over to relax and rejoice on your wedding day. In Chapter 3 we'll teach you the basics of diamonds and ring styles and help you find a wedding ring that you'll be happy to wear for the rest of your life. Chapters 4 and 5 will help you find the perfect location for your event and inspire you to spread the word about your wedding with creativity and style. Chapter 6 is focused on the special role of the bride, and Chapter 7 is all about the responsibilities of the groom and the fun and unique ways he can get involved in the wedding planning process. In Chapters 8 through 19 we'll share everything we know about the different aspects of planning a one-of-a-kind wedding with help from all the right professionals, and finally, in our Resources section, we'll provide you with a multitude of informative links so you can use this book in conjunction with the Internet and find additional tools, advice, and recommendations that may relate to your specific interests.

This book was created in a highly visual format to show off what makes weddings beautiful and to spark your imagination. The images come from some of the world's leading wedding photographers. Some were taken in the studio, and many were taken at real weddings much like the one

you're planning. We hope these photos will inform and inspire you!

The text was written to encourage you to have your wedding, your way, and to help ensure that when it's all over you'll have fond memories and zero regrets. Each chapter has color-coded tabs to make specific information easy to find and each page is full of practical information, as well as inspirational ideas.

You may read this book cover to cover or refer to relevant chapters or spreads as needed. We suggest you begin with Chapters 1 and 2 to get off on the right foot and then choose the topics you're most interested in from there. You'll notice that some pages have sidebars, which showcase helpful advice that's also color-coded for ease of use. Here's how they work:

Make it easy: Simple tools, techniques, and how-to advice

Zoom: Detailed information, definitions, and facts

Red light: Decisions you may want to stop and give some extra thought to

Yellow light: Simple rules of etiquette to help guide you on your way

Green light: Great ideas and ecofriendly wedding practices

Handwritten notes: A little extra information about the ideas illustrated in the photos

We wish you all the best in your wedding planning journey, and to further ensure your success, we hope you'll visit our Web site, JunebugWeddings.com. There you'll find an array of helpful wedding planning articles, inspiration, and advice. We have recommendations of the best wedding professionals, a blog that features new products and ideas daily, fashion reports showcasing the latest bridal trends, a library of gorgeous real weddings from around the world, and groombug, an informative section just for the guys. We know your wedding will be a one-of-a-kind celebration that's totally you, and we're thrilled and honored to lend our support.

YOUR WEDDING, YOUR WAY

Stress-free wedding planning tips to help you have your cake and eat it, too!

There are millions of ways to creatively express your love and celebrate your marriage. Finding your own way can be one of the most rewarding things about wedding planning—and one of the most challenging. You want to hang on to the euphoria you felt when you first got engaged without having it turn into worries about planning your wedding. So

before you begin to make the many choices that will make your big day unique, stop and spend some special time with your partner, focusing on these simple steps to stress-free wedding planning.

Step one: Share your dreams and expectations of what it means to have a wedding. Talk about the people and

Congratulations, You're Engaged!

© photo by GH Kim Photography

- You said "Yes!" You've made a commitment to spend the rest of your lives together. Revel in the reality of how lucky you are before you begin making plans.

- Say "I love you" and count the ways. Let your partner

know that you're thrilled to be getting married and share all the reasons you think this is the best decision for your life. It will do you both good to hear it.

Share Your Dreams

© photo by J. Garner Photography

- Really listen and share to find out what's important to you and the one you love.

- Chances are you'll be delighted, surprised, and occasionally challenged by what you find out, so stay curious and open-minded.

- Share some stories about weddings you've attended. Focus on the elements that made each of them unique. What parts did you appreciate and find really special, and what parts didn't you personally connect with?

traditions you want to honor and the things you're looking forward to.

Step two: Make a top-ten list that emphasizes what each of you considers most important about your wedding day. Then share your lists with each other. Understanding each other's dreams will help you make decisions you'll feel good about when you get married and throughout your years together.

Step three: Once you have your priorities set, decide on a wedding date and whom you want to tell about your engagement and when to tell them. Consider making your announcement special by hosting an engagement party, sharing it at a family event, or putting it in the paper or on a Web site.

Step four: Last but not least, have fun finding ways to celebrate your preferences, your backgrounds, and your differences. Use your love and imagination to find new ways to work together. Remember: The partnering skills you'll learn while planning your wedding will be a gift you'll both be grateful for as you share your lives together.

Share Your Good News

© photo by GH Kim Photography

- The hustle and bustle of wedding planning is on its way, so be sure to savor the romance of the moment and celebrate this big step together.

- Agree on a plan for sharing your news before you start.

- Tell both sets of parents at the same time and before anyone else. Hearing the big news directly from you will be important to them.

- Share your news with family, close friends, and acquaintances—in that order.

Celebrate for Years to Come

© photo by Yours by John Photography

- Start living your vows now. Take advantage of opportunities to demonstrate the commitment "for better or worse, for richer or poorer" as you plan your wedding.

- Make keeping perspective a family tradition. Give your wedding the weight it deserves without getting weighed down by it.

- Make a pact to keep your romance alive now and forever, no matter how busy you get. Designate at least one night a week as "date night" and give your partner your undivided attention.

SEASONAL STYLE
Seasonal touches inspired by nature bring a special sense of time and place to your celebration

No matter what style suits you best, using seasonal accents in your wedding design will help you create a memorable sense of time and place. In addition, choosing fresh, locally grown foods and flowers will reduce your impact on the environment in uniquely delicious and beautiful ways. Discover what you each love most about the season, and celebrate it.

In the spring choose bright yellow daffodils and lipstick pink tulips for your bouquet, and every year when they begin to bloom you'll be reminded that your anniversary is on its way. Have a fresh floral wreath made for your flower girl's hair, use a bird's nest for a ring pillow, or incorporate fashion accessories for your wedding wardrobe in shades of

Spring Style

© photo by GH Kim Photography

Summer Style

© photo by J. Garner Photography

- Paper parasols and antique umbrellas keep spring rain at bay and look sweet and romantic in photos.

- Lacy loose bouquets of peonies and potted centerpieces of mini daffodils, crocuses, and reticulated irises shout out spring style.

- Baby carrots, young asparagus, new potatoes, and sugar snap peas evoke the season and taste delicious.

- Baroque arrangements from composers like Handel and Vivaldi, with an emphasis on trumpets and horns, herald a spring bride down the aisle.

- Big bright bouquets of sunflowers, dahlias, and delphinium, or fragrant blossoms like roses, stephanotis, and gardenias, show off the season.

- Decorative metal buckets and watering cans filled with blossoms make smart centerpieces and fun take-

- home gifts for your family members and bridal party.

- Don't forget a change of shoes or two to help soothe your hot feet. And carry a powder puff or blotting papers to keep your face and neck pretty and shine free.

robin's egg blue, soft green, or petal pink.

In the heat of the summer, serve up slices of delicious wedding cake filled with fresh berries and other ripe fruit, and accompany them with cold mint juleps, passion fruit punch, or tart lemonade. Have your ceremony programs made up as pretty paper fans to keep your guests cool in the hot summer sun.

For fall play up the harvest season with floral arrangements that include fall leaves and berries. Choose rich oranges, reds, and russets for your color palette. Treat your guests to a hearty buffet of seasonal fresh vegetables, savory entrees,

and warm crusty breads, and serve hot apple cider or mulled spiced wine to keep everyone cozy.

Go glam in winter with a black-and-white wedding with splashes of ruby red or emerald green. Find a gorgeous faux-fur wrap to cover your shoulders, or have one designed to match your wedding dress. Hold a candlelight ceremony and decorate your reception with thousands of twinkling lights. Give personalized mugs complete with packets of rich cocoa, chocolate spoons, and mini marshmallows as take-home favors for your guests to enjoy.

Fall Style

© photo by Barbie Hull Photography

- Wineries, orchards, and historic barns are fabulous locations for fall weddings.

- Homemade preserves, maple syrup, and caramel apples make fun additions to the menu and thoughtful take-home favors.

- Walkways with luminarias

or jack-o'-lanterns with welcoming faces look lovely on an autumn night.

- Serve pie instead of wedding cake or as an additional dessert. Who doesn't love pumpkin and pecan pie or a warm apple tart with a dollop of vanilla bean ice cream?

Winter Style

© photo by GH Kim Photography

- Ski lodges, mansions, and intimate venues with fireplaces and dark wood accents feel warm and snug on cold winter days.

- Use crystals, shiny sugar, and gold and silver decorations in your decor. Give silver dinner bells away as favors.

- Keep winter travel to a minimum by having your reception near your ceremony or at the same place.

- Don't forget the mistletoe! Hang it in every doorway to put guests in an affectionate mood.

GETTING STARTED

Get ready, get set, and get started planning your wedding day with ideas that inspire you

You're about to plan one of the most elaborate and momentous events of your life. You'll need lots of support, solid advice, and a flexible attitude to make the most of it. To get off on the right foot, begin by creating your guest list. Make a "must have" list of all the people you simply have to have with you, and a "wish" list of those it would be fun to invite.

Soon, when many of your budget decisions come down to "per head" estimates, you can easily compare the two lists and weigh your options.

Create a spreadsheet to help keep your guest list organized. Include contact information and add columns to record your RSVPs, the gifts you give and receive, when you send out

Create Your Guest List

© photo by La Vie Photography

- Begin your guest list with your families. This might seem like a given, but they have to eat too, and they'll figure in your head count.

- If your heart is set on a particular venue, find out how many people the site accommodates before you finalize your list.

- Focus on people who love and support you; after all, they're the VIPs in your life.

- Keep in mind that the average wedding costs between $100 and $150 per person.

Get Organized

WEDDING VENDORS

GUEST LIST

WEDDING BUDGET

© photo by Junebug Weddings

- Staying organized is the key to event success. If keeping organized is not your strong suit, hiring a planner to help you will be invaluable.

- Include a timeline, a seating chart, your budget, your guest list, and your priority

- list in your organizer. Don't forget to refer to your budget and your priority list as you make decisions.

- Keep copies of all your contracts and deposit receipts in order and in a safe place.

your thank-you notes, and miscellaneous information like your bridal party's measurements or which guests need a vegetarian meal.

Buy, or put together, a wedding planner with lots of pocket folders and room to grow. Label separate folders for every vendor you plan to hire—one for color charts, one for fabric swatches, at least one for your fashion ideas, and several more to fill up with inspirational ideas, photos, and magazine tear sheets. Take your binder with you to tastings, tours, and meetings with professionals.

Search the Internet for resources and start a favorites list on your computer to quickly find the wedding Web sites and blogs that you love. Look to the Resource Directory of this book to find other helpful and creative wedding resources available online. Treat yourself to the books and magazines that you're drawn to; put your feet up, read, relax, and let yourself dream.

Create a pretty scrapbook later from the items in your planner.

Get Inspired

© photo by Junebug Weddings

- Create a collage of images or an "inspiration board" that you can refer to when explaining your wedding style vision to the professionals you're working with.

- Inspiration comes from an endless variety of sources. Let yourself be inspired by your favorite color, song, or hobby, or take inspiration from your family and your faith.

- Visit JunebugWeddings.com and other wedding blogs and Web sites and get inspired to create a wedding that's all about you.

Create an Heirloom

© photo by Junebug Weddings

- Arrange your pre-wedding photos, letters, and sketches, including tickets and mementos from favorite dates and trips.

- Record stories that you don't want to forget. Include kind gestures, helpful advice, and funny things that happen along the way.

- Showcase the color swatches, fabrics, and fashion and design photos that inspired you.

- Finish off your scrapbook with a copy of your vows, your signed marriage license, and a picture of your kiss.

SETTING YOUR BUDGET

Create a budget based on your priorities that both of you will be comfortable with

Creating an organized budget is a necessity. Start by determining who will be hosting and contributing to your wedding and then add together all the available resources. Chances are the two of you will pay for much of it with help from your parents, but every family is different, so that is far from a given. Whether or not your parents decide to be financially involved, they may have people they want included in your guest list. Meet with your families and show them your guest list as well as the top three items from each of your priority lists so they'll know what's important to you.

The average wedding in the United States today costs $25,000 and includes approximately 170 guests. That's

Who's Hosting?

© photo by La Vie Photography

- Traditionally a bride's parents paid for her wedding, but this is no longer the norm.

- If your parents will be involved financially, ask them to contribute a set amount rather than pay for certain items. It will make it easier for you to allocate expenses.

- No matter who ends up paying, your wedding is still a family affair. Be sure you take into consideration the desires of those closest to you.

The Average Wedding Budget

© photo by Junebug Weddings

- Up to 50 percent of your wedding budget will be spent on your reception.

- Other big-ticket items will include your wedding fashions, music, flowers, and photography.

- Allocate funds for each service, and if you go over on one, subtract from another.

- Almost half of all weddings go over budget, so take care of unforeseen expenses by building in an extra 10 to 15 percent before you begin spending.

around $150 per person. You may not flinch at that figure at all, but if you do, don't worry; we'll give you lots of suggestions for saving money without sacrificing style.

To stay organized and within your budget, open up a separate bank account for your expenditures and record all of your transactions in a spreadsheet. Update it regularly and review it together throughout the planning process.

YELLOW LIGHT

If you plan on getting a loan to pay for your wedding, a good rule of thumb is to not spend more than you can pay off in a year. Avoid opening new credit cards, save wisely, and give yourself another reason to celebrate your first anniversary: being free of wedding debt!

Personalize Your Spreadsheet

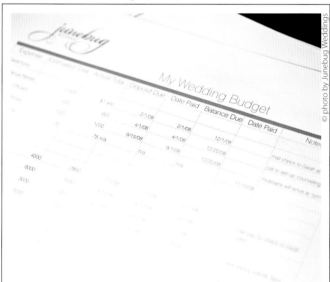

© photo by Junebug Weddings

- To stay on budget you'll have to stay organized, so have your budget spreadsheet ready before you begin spending money.

- Create a spreadsheet for your guest list and your budget. Keep track of how many people RSVP to help finalize your budget.

- Set aside time once a week to update your spreadsheets and create an electronic backup of all the wedding information you have stored on your computer.

Manage Your Debt

© photo by J. Garner Photography

- If you're already homeowners and need a wedding loan, look for a home-equity line with no prepayment penalty before using a credit card.

- If you do need to use a credit card, search for a low-interest option that offers some sort of reward.

- Consider creative ways you can add to your income instead of borrowing.

- Use the money management techniques you learn now to build a strong foundation for the future.

CREATING YOUR TIMELINE

First things first: eight to twelve months before your wedding

Among the many details involved in wedding planning are a few foundational elements that set the stage for all the others. Start with these important decisions and you'll be ready to move forward and plan, stress free.

Set your date. Ideally, you'll give yourself twelve months or longer to plan your wedding. Begin by choosing a date that's easy on you and your guests. Then consider hiring a consultant. Wedding consultants are available for every aspect of planning, from complete coordination to "day of" assistance. Plus, experienced consultants have the knowledge and expertise to help you save time and money while giving you the confidence to pull off a memorable event.

Book your reception venue. Once you've chosen an overall style or theme for your wedding, you'll want to search for a

Set Your Date

© photo by Positive Light Photography

- Choose a date in your favorite season, or one of emotional significance, like the day you first met or first kissed.

- Before you set your date in stone, check with the people most important to you and be sure they're available to attend.

- If you start planning a little late, or if you're on a tight budget, consider having your wedding on a date other than Saturday, when locations and vendors will be more available.

Hire a Consultant

© photo by La Vie Photography

- The average wedding takes over 250 hours to plan. If your time is valuable, hiring a consultant can be a highly practical use of funds.

- Savvy consultants know how to negotiate contracts and cut costs on things you and your guests will never miss.

- Many couples say that hiring a consultant was their best wedding planning decision.

- Interview at least three different consultants and consider their professionalism, experience, and personalities.

venue that really shows it off. Your venue will be the key to setting the tone for your wedding day. The cost to rent your reception site, combined with catering expenses, is bound to be your largest expenditure, so don't get overwhelmed. Schedule time for your ceremony and rehearsal, and be sure to add one to two hours to your allotted ceremony time for pictures and unforeseen delays.

Book your officiant. Find someone you like and respect and who shares your beliefs. Then schedule any required counseling appointments.

Find your photographer and videographer. We know that when it's all said and done, you'll look to your wedding photos for your memories and you'll pass them on to future generations. Don't underestimate the importance of hiring a pro for this important job. Popular photographers' and videographers' schedules fill up quickly, so book them well in advance and be ready to give them a deposit along with your contract to secure your wedding date.

Choose Your Locations

© photo by GH Kim Photography

- Popular venues can book up years in advance, so don't delay in making this important decision.

- Book your officiant along with your ceremony site. Some sites require certain officiants, and some officiants won't travel to perform ceremonies.

- Conduct site inspections of your locations. Take traffic flow, parking, rental needs, and lighting into consideration.

- Calculate the distance between your ceremony and your reception site and have a plan for group transportation if necessary.

Find Your Photographer

© photo by La Vie Photography

- Compare at least three photographers for style, price, and personality.

- Schedule any additional photography time for your rehearsal dinner or engagement photos when you book your wedding.

- Create a photo album for your guy that he's guaranteed to love. Schedule a tasteful boudoir photo session and show off your playful, sexy side.

- Consider asking your photographer for vendor recommendations; their unique perspectives can be priceless.

CREATING YOUR TIMELINE

Planning a day to remember: four to eight months before your wedding

Here's where life gets busy and super fun! You're about to decide what you'll be wearing, how to announce your wedding day, and what you'll be offering your guests, from food to music to atmosphere.

Have some fun and dive right into your fashion fantasies to find a dress that makes you feel like a million bucks. Arrange to have any necessary alterations started immediately to avoid last-minute hassles. Choose your bridal party and get your girls together to brainstorm their fashions. Get busy putting together the rest of your wedding look, from your shoes to your hairstyle to your accessories, and be sure your man is busy putting his look together as well.

Fashion Your Look

© photo by GH Kim Photography

- The transformation of a woman into a bride is simply breathtaking. Revel in your moment by creating a look that makes you feel confident, poised, and totally gorgeous.

- Buy your dress first, then your shoes and your veil. Most wedding dress boutiques require appointments, so be sure to call ahead.

- Make appointments for day-before manis and pedis and day-of hair and makeup services when you first book your stylists.

Create Your Menu

© photo by GH Kim Photography

- Determine the type of meal you'll be serving based on the time of your reception, and then choose the formality of the service. A seated dinner with a full waitstaff is the height of classic elegance, but it's substantially more costly than a buffet-style brunch.

- Nearly anything is available to rent, so look for stylish options for your dishes, linens, chairs, portable dance floors, and lighting.

- If you want an elaborate custom cake, book your designer now.

If you haven't hired an in-house caterer through your reception site, meet with caterers now. Decide on a menu that harmonizes with your style and fits your budget, and be sure you understand exactly what's included in your contract. Order any additional rental items that you'll need like tables, chairs, dishes, dance floors, and lighting.

Once you've sewn up the questions of where, when, and what to serve your guests, choose any and all of the musicians, DJs, and entertainers you're planning on having.

Meet with an invitation designer or pick out your paper products online. Remember to mail your save-the-dates six months ahead to guests who'll need to make travel arrangements.

Hire your florist. Flowers are an important piece of your wedding decor and your fashion ensemble. Choose someone who is creative and passionate about helping you express your style.

Book hotel rooms for yourself and your guests. Negotiate a package price for a block of rooms, and if you're having a destination wedding, make these arrangements as early as possible.

Design Your Invitations

© photo by Junebug Weddings

- Meet with at least three designers and bring your address list and details about your wedding style, theme, and colors with you.

- Ask your stationer if he or she can help you with wording and hand addressing envelopes.

- Be clear about who will be responsible if mistakes are made in the printing process.

- Order your invitations along with your other paper decor, from save-the-dates to thank-you cards, to help save time and printing setup fees.

Hire Your Florist

© photo by La Vie Photography

- Determine whether you'll need a florist or a floral designer. A florist will provide you with arrangements, and a floral designer will transform your venue with floral decor.

- Take your color palette, fabric swatches, a picture of your dress, and a list of the flowers that you love with you to your meetings.

- Communicate your budget requirements up front, but don't eliminate a company that you love simply because the first quote doesn't work. Thoroughly discuss alternatives and options.

CREATING YOUR TIMELINE

Pull together your plan and fill in the details: two to four months before your wedding

In the next few months, you'll be putting the finishing touches on your planning to ensure that your big day unfolds gracefully. If you haven't already, set up a time to taste cakes and desserts. Take your mom or friends with you to add to the fun. If you're not cake lovers, consider getting a small one just for cutting, or choose another sweet dessert alternative.

Pick out your wedding bands and shop for gifts. Make a day of it and have fun choosing these things together. While your mind is on gifts, be sure to register for items of your own. Give your guests a wide range of options to suit every budget.

Check in with each other to be sure you're each taking care

Order Your Cake

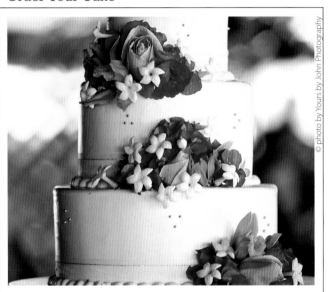

© photo by Yours by John Photography

- Wedding cakes come in a mouthwatering array of delicious flavors and fillings and an endless array of styles, usually ranging from $2 to $12 per slice.

- Attend a tasting to try out samples of cake flavors and see photos of other cakes the designer has made.

- To guarantee that your cake is as delicious as it is beautiful, be sure it will be served fresh and never frozen and ask your baker for a list of the ingredients that he or she uses.

Buy Wedding Bands and Gifts

© photo by GH Kim Photography

- Decide if you'll be buying matching bands or each choosing your own style.

- While there are good companies online to buy your wedding bands from, it's safest to buy from a reputable local dealer who has at least ten years' experience in business.

- Allow eight to ten weeks for special-order gifts and engravings.

- Check your registry as things unfold to be sure a wide range of gift options and price options remain.

of your specific responsibilities, but don't ask for too many details; there may be fun surprises in the works!

Be sure you have your paperwork in order. Research and complete the marriage license requirements for your state, renew your passport if traveling, and schedule any necessary blood tests or vaccinations. If you'll be changing your name, consider waiting until you get back from your honeymoon. Air travel may require the name used at the time of booking.

As time unfolds, confirm every reservation and detail. Meet with your caterer, give your DJ your playlist, and send your photographer and videographer a list of important shots. Go to final fittings to ensure you're dressed to impress and make appointments for your manicure, pedicure, makeup, and hairstyle.

Last but not least, send out your invitations. Eight weeks is the perfect amount of time for nearby guests to make arrangements for your wedding. Remember to have thank-you notes ready as your RSVPs and wedding gifts roll in.

Fill Out Your Paperwork

- For marriage license requirements and name change information, see our Resources section.

- Make a list of financial items that you'll need to address, including merging bank accounts, mortgage documents, and insurance information.

- Sit down together and run a complete credit report on each other's financial profiles before you merge your assets.

- If you have concerns about existing property or inheritances, consider a prenup. They're not just for celebrities.

Invite Your Guests

- Addressing invitations is exacting and time-consuming. Consider hiring your invitation designer or a calligrapher to assist. Formal and semiformal invitations should be hand addressed.

- Send your photographer your invitation so it can be photographed.

- Set up a wedding Web site for your guests. Post your wedding schedule, tourist information, driving directions, and fun, personal content. See our Resources section for a list of wedding Web site services available.

CREATING YOUR TIMELINE

Put the finishing touches on your wedding plans: two months to one day before your wedding

You're almost there! As your wedding day approaches, you'll be preparing for your ceremony and reception, shopping for your honeymoon, going to parties, and getting gorgeous. Have a blast and stay organized!

Finalize the details of your ceremony. Meet with your officiant to discuss your schedule and review processional and recessional arrangements. Write and rehearse your vows, confirm musicians and readers, and set aside your programs to be delivered to ushers two days before your wedding day.

Visualize your reception. Write your toast and practice it, and be sure your best man and other speakers are prepared as well. Schedule dance lessons and take two a week until

Plan Ceremony Events

© photo by La Vie Photography

- Think through your entire ceremony from start to finish and don't forget the ending. Your exit provides an opportunity for a really fun send-off and a great photo op. Choose birdseed, bubbles, sparklers, or bells to give out to your guests.

- Make a list of extra items you'll need during your ceremony. Include things like your Ketubah, a glass to break, a unity candle, a lucky penny for your shoe, and your interpretation of "something old, something new."

Plan Reception Events

© photo by Yours by John Photography

- Double check that your reception site or DJ will provide the necessary sound equipment for music as well as speeches.

- Make a list of the extra items you'll need at your reception, like wedding favors, special gifts, a garter for throwing, and a guest book.

- Give your caterer and venue manager your final head count.

- Confirm set-up and tear-down details and obtain any necessary permits or insurance.

you're ready to glide into your first dance. Consider buying toasting glasses or a special knife to cut your cake. Make the most of your lighting; be sure it plays up your decor and showcases your reception events.

Enjoy your parties! Schedule your rehearsal dinner and other wedding-related events. Have fun at your bachelor and bachelorette parties and enjoy socializing with friends from near and far. Their presence is a gift.

Send out your thank-you notes and express your gratitude generously. Do your best to get handwritten notes out within two weeks of receiving gifts, and be sure you have your thank-you gifts wrapped and ready to go.

Remember to pamper yourself every day along the way. Drink lots of water, eat well, take your vitamins, and go to the gym more often than not. Enjoy visits to the spa, get a series of facials, and take care of your hands and feet. Run through your complete wedding-day look, to be sure you're not forgetting anything. Get rid of tan lines, whiten your teeth, and let yourself smile!

Say Thank You

© photo by La Vie Photography

- Give gifts to your bridal party at your rehearsal dinner or wait until you get home from your honeymoon; either is appropriate.

- Tickets to favorite shows and sports events are great gifts you can share with your friends.

- Gifts like good luck charms, jewelry, or watches are reminders of your appreciation that will last a lifetime.

- Show your appreciation by being on time and smartly dressed for all parties and showers in your honor.

Pamper Yourself and Get Gorgeous

© photo by J. Garner Photography

- Brides, be sure to take your veil, hair accessories, and jewelry with you to the salon for a trial runthrough of your hair and makeup.

- Grooms, don't discount the relaxing and rejuvenating power of a good massage or spa treatment. They're not just for the girls!

- Get plenty of rest the week before your big day, even though there are lots of things to do to keep you extra busy.

DIAMONDS

A little knowledge goes a long way when choosing the perfect diamond for your engagement ring

Just like snowflakes and people, each diamond is different. To find one that stands out from the crowd, shop at a reputable store that carries independently certified diamonds complete with warranties and educate yourself about the four Cs.

Cut: The shape of the diamond you choose, whether it be round, square, emerald, or marquise, is a matter of preference.

The way a diamond is cut is a matter of skill. Even a moderately priced diamond in the hands of a skilled jeweler can become a stone of mesmerizing brilliance. To ensure your diamond makes the cut, choose a certified stone that's rated good, very good, premium, or ideal.

Color: Diamond colors start at the extremely rare and

Cut

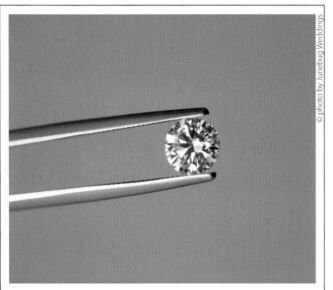

© photo by Junebug Weddings

- The most popular diamond today is the 58-facet round, similar to the diamond in this photo. Some jewelers offer finer cuts that have dozens of additional facets to increase light refraction.

- The depth of a diamond's cut affects its brilliance. Diamonds that are cut too

- deep or too shallow lose brilliance from the bottom and can appear dark and muddy.

- Look at your diamond under natural light to see its true brilliance. The artificial lights used in most retail stores can be misleading.

Color

© photo by Junebug Weddings

- While colorless diamonds are rare and expensive, many people like diamonds in the faint yellow category. You can see the slight difference in the stones above.

- Buy in person to ensure you get what you pay for and like what you see.

- Beware of fancy names for yellow and brown diamonds. They are often used as a sales gimmick to sell diamonds of lower quality.

- A few very rare diamonds come in colors like pink, green, gold, and red.

colorless grade D and continue through the alphabet to the light yellow grade Z. The more truly colorless a stone is, the more you can expect to pay for it.

Clarity: The clarity of a diamond refers to the impact of its inclusions, tiny imperfections that can affect the way it reflects light. The fewer inclusions, the more expensive the stone.

Carat: The carat is the weight of a diamond. For some folks it's the size of the rock that matters; for others it's the cut, color, or sentimental value.

ZOOM

An internationally adopted certification process called the Kimberley Process now ensures diamonds are conflict free in over forty-eight countries, so couples no longer have to worry about buying a "blood diamond" that contributes to global strife. To find out more visit www.diamondfacts.org.

Clarity

© photo by Junebug Weddings

- Look at your diamond under a GemScope with 10x magnification and ask if the diamond has been filled to hide imperfections.

- Diamond clarity ranges from flawless down to several levels of imperfect.

- Flawless gems are extremely expensive, so keep in mind that inclusions seen only under 10x or greater magnification cannot be seen by the naked eye.

- Buy based on what you see, not based on what a salesperson tells you.

Carat

© photo by Junebug Weddings

- Most grooms buy engagement diamonds for about one to three months of their salary. We suggest you spend whatever you're comfortable with.

- Be sure to have your diamond weight verified before you make your purchase.

- Ask your jeweler if your diamond is "Kimberley Certified" and ask to see documentation.

- Remember: There is no correlation between the size of a diamond and the happiness of a marriage.

ENGAGEMENT RINGS
Find an engagement ring you'll love to wear for the rest of your life

Ever since the 1940s, diamond engagement rings have been the choice for couples in love all over the world. The styles have changed with the fashions, but a dazzling rock on a lady's left hand has become an enduring symbol of love and commitment.

Today the most popular diamonds are round cut, largely because their shape is ideal for multifaceted cutting that creates brilliance. However, emerald-cut, pear-shaped, and square-cut diamonds are all notably classic styles.

In addition to the shape, the setting for your diamond has enormous impact on its style. While a round diamond in a six-prong setting on a thin round band looks decidedly classic, the same diamond in a modern setting can look dramatically different.

Classic

© photo by Junebug Weddings

- There's nothing more classic than a diamond solitaire mounted on a thin band of white gold or platinum.

- In 1886 Tiffany introduced the six-prong solitaire diamond engagement ring and it quickly caught fire with the elite.

- Keep in mind that a woman's engagement ring is first and foremost an emotional investment. With a little luck and a lot of love, she'll wear it every day for the rest of her life and never dream of selling it.

Modern

© photo by Junebug Weddings

- Raised settings lift the diamond high above the band; tension settings, like the one above, are dramatic and architectural; flush settings are simple and clean; and all are gorgeous modern design options.

- Modern engagement ring styles have the appeal of clean lines and easy elegance.

- When choosing a setting consider your lifestyle. While beautiful, settings that elevate a stone can catch on things, and intricately detailed settings can be hard to keep clean.

Raised settings with clean modern lines look contemporary, and rings with smoothly twisted or intricately wrought settings evoke an aura of glamour.

Using multiple stones in a ring can boost the sparkle and often reduce the price. For instance, a 1-carat diamond next to two .5-carat diamonds looks impressive and can cost significantly less than a single 2-carat stone.

Recently pavé (pronounced pah-vay), or diamond-encrusted, rings have become all the rage. These rings are covered with small sparkling diamonds that reflect light from every direction.

Multiple Stones

© photo by Junebug Weddings

- Rings with multiple stones have an opulent, romantic look.

- Creating a custom ring from your family diamonds is a lovely way to create a sentimental treasure with modern style.

- Some couples choose to add stones to their original ring on a major anniversary or when they're better able to afford something more expensive.

- Consider adding rubies, emeralds, or sapphires to a multiple-stone ring to give it a more complex look.

Decorative Detailing

© photo by Junebug Weddings

- This pavé ring has a bezel setting. Small diamonds surround the main stone, creating an illusion of having a larger diamond.

- *Pavé* literally means "paved" with diamonds.

- Round and princess-cut diamonds are frequently used in pavé-style rings because the surrounding stones create sufficient brilliance to make fancier cuts unnecessary.

- Pavé diamonds can circle the entire band or just the front half, leaving the inside half bare for comfort and savings.

WITH THIS RING

WEDDING BANDS
With this ring you will wed, so find one that matches your style

The ancient Egyptians were the first to wear wedding rings on the third finger of their left hand to symbolize betrothal. The vein running down that finger was believed to lead straight to the heart, and the circle signified love's eternal nature. These symbols still endure today in the wedding ring ceremonies of countless cultures throughout the world.

Unlike ancient rings of leather, bone, and iron, today's rings are made from precious metals fashioned to last a lifetime. Strong, durable platinum has remained the most popular metal for rings since the 1950s, but because of its skyrocketing price, white gold and yellow gold are making their way back to the market with lovely results.

While most modern rings are smooth simple circles, many new and custom designs as well as vintage and antique rings

Gold

© photo by Junebug Weddings

- Gold rings are imprinted with their karat designation of 24 karat, 18 karat, or 14 karat.

- Twenty-four karat gold is the most precious, but also the most malleable, and 14 karat rings are less expensive but more durable.

- Gold rings are hypoallergenic, so almost anyone can wear them with little or no negative reaction.

- White gold is sturdier than yellow gold and is often used as a substitute for platinum. White gold is available in 18 karat or 14 karat only.

Platinum

© photo by Junebug Weddings

- The white luster of platinum is beautiful in even the simplest designs.

- Platinum is a rare and durable precious metal that looks lovely with any stone and on any skin tone.

- Thirty times stronger than gold, platinum rings stand the test of time and don't corrode.

- Because of its rarity, Louis XVI declared it to be "the only metal fit for a king" back in the 1780s.

feature multiple stones, intricate filigree, or symbolic ornamentation, so no matter what your style, you'll have plenty of options when it comes to choosing the one that's right for you. To ensure you find the one ring you'll be as happy with in fifty years as you are on your wedding day, choose one that complements the size of your hand and the length of your fingers and is as comfortable as it is beautiful.

Rings enchanted with the power to protect the wearer have been at the center of folklore throughout recorded history. So it's not surprising that the rings used in today's ceremonies, both Christian and otherwise, are blessed by the officiant, thus continuing the practice of infusing the rings with protective powers.

Eternity Bands

© photo by Junebug Weddings

- Eternity rings have a continuous stream of gems around the band.

- Wide bands encrusted with diamonds look stunning on long slim fingers, and thin rings with delicate detailing look lovely on small hands.

- Although all eternity bands are similar by definition, there are numerous styles available; some look modern and some romantic.

- Some women wear an eternity band instead of an engagement ring or traditional wedding band, while some wear all three.

Alternative Styles

© photo by Junebug Weddings

- Wide decorative bands like this one make a dramatic impact and can cost far less than a diamond solitaire and wedding band set.

- Men's and women's wedding bands don't have to coordinate perfectly. There's no reason you can't mix and match metals and stones.

- Make a special date to buy your rings and settle on ones you both adore.

- If you can dream about it, a jeweler can make it. Play up your jewelry fantasies with a custom ring design.

29

ANTIQUE & VINTAGE RINGS

Family heirlooms, antiques, and vintage rings are romantic and sentimental

Choosing an antique wedding ring to represent your marriage commitment is a perfect style choice for the ultimate romantic. Each one-of-a-kind piece has a personality all its own and a long, rich history. The stones were cut to reflect low candlelight; the delicate details were shaped, cut, and pierced by hand; and each ring's originality lives on today.

If your wedding ring is a family heirloom, take it to a jeweler who specializes in antiques to have it cleaned, inspected for damage, and restored the correct way. When shopping for an antique wedding ring, explore the pieces available from reputable jewelers and choose one that speaks to your heart. With antique jewelry, you're investing in more than just the

Edwardian

© photo by Junebug Weddings

- Decorative scrollwork, lace-like filigree, flower garlands, bows, and tassels are characteristic of Edwardian designs.

- The Edwardian period (1901–1910) was named for England's King Edward VII and was also called the Belle Époque.

- Platinum's strength and light color made it the metal of choice for the popular white-on-white color palette.

- Old mine-cut and European-cut diamonds, as well as pearls, were delicately set to look like they were floating.

Art Deco

© photo by Junebug Weddings

- Art deco rings have bold architectural and geometric designs with strong angles and straight lines.

- The art deco style was popular post–World War I, in the roaring 1920s through the late 1930s.

- Egyptian, Asian, and Indian motifs; the Machine Age; and modern art like the Cubist movement and the Ballet Russe inspired fashion and jewelry trends.

- Engagement rings had old mine-cut or Asscher-cut center diamonds, with side accent stones in baguette or geometric shapes.

technical aspects of your ring, but you should still ask for independent appraisal documentation to educate yourself about what you're buying.

Ring styles have varied throughout history, and the time period in which your ring was made is a fascinating connection to the past. Changes in politics, economics, and technology led to changes in fashion and standards of beauty. Most antique jewelry available for purchase today begins with Edwardian-style rings from the early 1900s and moves up through the art nouveau, art deco, and retro styles.

············ GREEN ● LIGHT ·············

Because the mining of metals and precious stones can wreak havoc on the environment and has been connected to a history of unjust labor practices, wearing an antique wedding ring is a fantastic way to be ecofriendly. You can be confident that no new materials were harvested for its creation.

Colored Stones

© photo by Junebug Weddings

- Richly colored gemstones like rubies, sapphires, and emeralds were used in rings throughout history.

- Diamond wedding rings didn't become standard until the mid-twentieth century.

- Light-colored gemstones like natural zircon, citrine, quartz, and aquamarine make glamorous alternatives to diamonds.

- Gemstones have always had special meanings. Among other things, emeralds represent faith, rubies represent passion, and sapphires represent intelligence.

Bands

© photo by Junebug Weddings

- Most antique bands weren't made as part of a set, so have fun with your selections and don't worry about them coordinating perfectly.

- Antique bands can contain colored stones, or no stones at all or be sparkling diamond eternity bands.

- Combining an eclectic mix of antique bands can be a fashion-forward way to wear an old-fashioned style.

- Antique bands can be so beautifully detailed that they look great even on their own.

WITH THIS RING

ALTERNATIVE STYLES

Set your own trend with an alternative ring that's just your style

There's no rule that says you need to wear a traditional diamond ring in order to say "I do." Just like your wedding ceremony and celebration, your ring should reflect your personal style and all the wonderful things your marriage means to you.

Take a cue from the jewelry you already wear and love, as well as the demands of your lifestyle. Do you love ultramodern designs with sleek, strong geometric shapes, or do you gravitate toward quirky, creative designs with asymmetric lines and rough-hewn edges? Do you work with your hands and need jewelry that can withstand the elements, or are delicate details right at home in your life?

Also consider different design factors to find the ring that's just right for you. Precious stones can be cut in many different ways, and their looks change greatly depending on the

Creative Cuts

© photo by Junebug Weddings

- New versions of rose-cut diamonds, like the ones above, combine a vintage sensibility with a modern style.

- Wedding rings with raw or rough-cut diamonds are interesting and understated alternatives to the classic diamond solitaire.

- Hand-faceted stones have a soft, organic look, while machine cuts are sharp and precise and give a stone its dramatic sparkle.

- A bezel setting, where the stone is surrounded by an even surface of metal instead of prongs, lends a modern look to any ring.

Alternative Colors

© photo by Junebug Weddings

- Choosing a wedding ring set with colored gemstones you love is a beautifully stylish and usually less-expensive option than a diamond ring.

- Colored diamonds are a fun twist on the traditional.

- Yellow gold is making a big resurgence with new looks created by high karat percentages and creative textures and finishes.

- Gold can be combined with other precious metals to create color shifts. Experiment with shades like rose, apricot, peach, and green gold.

way they reflect light. Metals and stones can have infinite color variations, too. Diamonds come in every shade of the rainbow, and gold and platinum change depending on the other metals they're mixed with and the way their surfaces are textured. Ring shapes can be large or small, traditional or inventive, and stacking multiple rings together allows you to wear your wedding rings in myriad different ways.

Nontraditional Shapes

© photo by Junebug Weddings

- Organic shapes that resemble wood, vines, and flowers are alternative yet ultrafeminine.

- Diamonds can be set in many creative ways. Pavé settings can cover large surface areas and bezel settings let stones float inside other materials.

- Wide bands with or without embellishments can be an easy-to-wear option instead of a traditional wedding set.

- Let your life inspire you. Rings can be designed to resemble everything from magnolia blossoms to microchips.

Stacking Multiple Rings

© photo by Junebug Weddings

- Stacking multiple small bands gives you flexibility to wear one ring at a time or all of them at once, depending on your activities.

- Mixing and matching colors, stones, metals, and textures creates a fun, funky, and eclectic look.

- Stacking sparkling diamond bands creates glamorous high-impact style.

- Wearing a number of simple bands is a great low-budget option and sets you up for a romantic future. Start with one now and add more for anniversaries or meaningful milestones.

WITH THIS RING

MEN'S RINGS
Masculine designs and precious metals stand the test of time

Men's wedding rings don't get as much attention as their female counterparts but are just as important nonetheless. They're the items that will physically represent your marriage to yourselves and to the outside world, and for many men they're the only pieces of jewelry they will own. Most men's rings are categorized by their width, ranging from three millimeters to eight millimeters, as well as the materials they're made from. Try on rings from every category to see which one looks and feels the best to you. For an item that's seemingly simple, there are lots of interesting options available.

Platinum became the most popular metal for jewelry in the early twentieth century and remains the favorite today. It's a strong, heavy precious metal that will look timeless

Platinum

© photo by Junebug Weddings

- Choose a high-polish finish or a brushed matte finish for your ring, or combine the two looks in one ring for more textural interest like in the image above.

- Platinum is very rare and therefore more precious and expensive than gold.

- Because of its strength and resistance to tarnish, wear, and corrosion, platinum is an ideal material for fine jewelry.

- Yellow gold and platinum can be used in the same ring, so you don't have to choose one look over the other.

Gold

© photo by Junebug Weddings

- Yellow gold comes in 14 karat, 18 karat, and 22 karat, getting softer and more richly yellow the higher the karat percentage.

- White gold is an alloy, made with a combination of 24-karat gold and either nickel or palladium.

- White gold can be coated with a thin layer of rhodium, a silvery white metal in the platinum group.

- Pay attention to the heft, height, and inside edges of your ring to be sure it will fit comfortably on your hand.

even when your children and grandchildren are shopping for their own weddings.

Gold and white gold are also classics, with white gold being the more popular for modern grooms. Because of the softness of gold, your ring will inevitably get scratched and scuffed. Take it back to your jeweler every few years for a polish or plating that will bring back its original luster.

With the prices of platinum and gold on the rise, less-expensive metals have become popular. Titanium and tungsten are both known for their strength and are far less expensive than platinum or gold. They can be difficult materials to work with, so not all jewelers are able to use them. They are usually not able to be sized or engraved, so keep that in mind when you make your purchase.

The designs of alternative rings are limited only by your own imagination. Buy from an independent designer, choose unusual patterns, add diamonds or gemstones, or get in on the design process yourself to create a ring unlike any other.

New Metals

© photo by Junebug Weddings

- This tungsten ring is heavier than a super-lightweight titanium one of the same size, and some men prefer the extra heft.

- Tungsten and tungsten-carbide rings are steel gray in color and are so hard they easily resist scratches and dings.

- Titanium is extremely strong, as well as light-weight, and is commonly used in the aerospace, sporting goods, and medical industries.

- Titanium does not react with the human body, so it's a good option for hyper-sensitive skin.

Alternative Styles

© photo by Junebug Weddings

- The top surface of your ring isn't the only area to work with. The side edges of these rings have been decorated, and the insides could be engraved.

- Popular patterns include milgrain edging, hand-hammered surfaces, or braided detailing.

- Different types of wood can be combined with metals and formed into unique wedding rings.

- Diamonds or other stones can be set in nontraditional ways for a casual, quirky, or especially masculine look.

CEREMONY BASICS

From a soaring cathedral to a country garden, choose a ceremony site that is just right for you

While over 75 percent of today's couples choose to get married in a church, synagogue, or mosque, any space that feels sacred to you can be the perfect place for your ceremony.

If you're members of a particular faith, then getting married at your house of worship may be your most comfortable choice. Talk to the on-site coordinator to book your date early

and be sure to get detailed information on any rules and regulations you'll have to follow, including required counseling appointments, guidelines for writing your vows, and restrictions on video recordings or photography. Ask if you can choose your officiant or if one will be designated for you.

If a traditional venue is not your first choice, then look for

Religious Ceremonies

© photo by La Vie Photography

Civil Ceremonies

© photo by La Vie Photography

- There are basically two types of ceremonies: civil and religious.

- Religious ceremonies incorporate rules of faith and require a religious officiant.

- If the officiant is willing to travel off site, a religious ceremony can be held at any venue that feels appropriate to you and your fiancé.

- The privacy of a ceremony inside a house of worship creates a sense of intimacy, ensures the safety of your guests, and limits unwanted distractions.

- The traditional civil ceremony takes place in a city hall but may take place at any location you love.

- Civil ceremonies require a legal official to marry you: a justice of the peace, judge, magistrate, county clerk, mayor, boat captain, or even a friend ordained online.

- If you're getting married for the second time, don't feel that you have to choose a civil ceremony. You're free to celebrate the way that feels best to you.

a private place with ambiance that matches your style and plenty of room for all of your guests. Most reception sites offer lovely on-site ceremony locations, with indoor and outdoor options, and beautiful beach, park, and garden ceremony sites abound.

To help secure your first choice, try to book your site and your officiant twelve to eighteen months before your wedding day.

Size and Space

© photo by GH Kim Photography

- Have a backup plan for wind and rain. If your guests will be required to sit outside for your ceremony or walk to your reception afterward, consider having lots of large umbrellas or parasols on hand, or look into tenting options. Tents, like the one above, can be beautiful.

- Keep in mind that you'll need about eight square feet per guest to accommodate people comfortably.

- If you'll be inviting guests with mobility needs, be sure your location is wheelchair accessible.

Special Considerations

© photo by La Vie Photography

- Check with your location in advance if you want to release birds, include your pets in the ceremony, or throw flower petals or birdseed.

- Think your ceremony through, from the moment you'll arrive until your last farewell. Be sure you have an easy place to park, a comfortable place to "hide" from guests, and a fun plan to make your grand exit.

- Be gentle with yourselves; the search for the right place and the right words can be a soul-searching experience.

CHOOSING A LOCATION

RECEPTION BASICS

Develop your perfect place profile to find a reception location that matches your style and budget

Choosing a location for your reception is one of the biggest decisions you'll make while planning your wedding. The size, style, and ambiance of your venue will set the mood for your event, while the catering and rental fees associated with it may easily add up to more than half of your budget. With an array of fabulous reception sites available, finding one that fits your style will probably be the fun and easy part of making your decision. However, settling on a venue that fits your budget and accommodates your choices can be much more complicated.

Many venues offer wedding packages that include catering, staffing, tableware, and linens, while some offer a huge

Choose the Setting

© photo by GH Kim Photography

- Decide if you're having your reception indoors, outdoors, or both, and pay careful attention to lighting options and restrictions.

- Choose a venue that can comfortably accommodate your guests. Plan to have eighteen square feet per person for your reception,

plus room for your dance floor and your DJ or band.

- Start your search by setting up appointments with catering managers or on-site coordinators. Notice how long it takes for the staff to return messages and how enthusiastic they are about your plans.

On Premises

© photo by GH Kim Photography

- Determine whether your location is an "on-premises" or "off-premises" venue.

- On-premises venues like hotel ballrooms come with a caterer and other event professionals, so be sure their options meet your expectations.

- Know what beverages you want to serve. The cost for beer and wine versus an open bar can greatly affect your costs.

- Keep in mind that all-inclusive packages can potentially save you lots of time and money.

selection of extras, including every aspect of event coordination from your cake to your music. Still others simply charge a facility rental fee and require that you do the rest. Determining which approach works best for you is crucial to making your decision. If you're thrilled with the ambiance, amenities, and vendor selection at an all-inclusive location, you may want to turn the details over to their staff. But if you're already set on a caterer and it's not the one they're providing, or if you're dreaming of a five-tiered chocolate cake with raspberries, and they offer only vanilla, you'll want some more

flexibility. From the start, determine what the location you're interested in provides and what restrictions apply. Get per-head quotes for a variety of options and take a good look at your guest list to see what each option adds up to.

To make a decision you'll truly be comfortable with, consider your budget as well as your priorities list, then schedule visits at several sites, ask the important questions listed below, and be ready to negotiate.

Off Premises

© photo by GH Kim Photography

- Alternative venues like art galleries, rustic farms, and urban lofts are fun examples of off-premises locations.

- Off-premises venues require you to hire professionals separately.

- Choosing your own professionals gives you greater control over the style and quality of your event.

- Even if you supply every item other than the space itself, there may still be fees charged for cake cutting, uncorking champagne, and overtime rental.

Other Considerations

© photo by GH Kim Photography

- Look for a venue with multiple locations for taking photos, and remember that every vista and architectural element is a potential backdrop.

- If you'll need to have a room "turned" from your ceremony to your reception space, be sure you have a

place to keep guests entertained during the transition.

- Don't underestimate amenities. Having spacious getting-ready rooms, extra bathrooms, and plenty of on-site parking can be a godsend on your wedding day.

39

CLASSIC LOCATIONS

Ballrooms, historic buildings, and private clubs are ideal places for formal receptions

For a reception venue that complements your classic style, look to hotels, private clubs, and sites of historic significance. The chandeliers, terraces, graceful stairways, and ornate decorations that frequently adorn these locations provide the ideal design elements for sophisticated events.

You'll find that many leading hotels offer beautiful ballrooms and dining halls designed specifically for formal events, complete with a professional staff and an on-site wedding coordinator to help with every detail of your planning. Many hotel packages are all-inclusive, meaning they provide your caterer, bartender, waitstaff, wedding cake, floral arrangements, and an array of tableware and decor items. This kind of complete

Elegant Touches

© photo by John and Joseph Photography

Glittering Ballrooms

© photo by GH Kim Photography

- Gorgeous window-lit stairways make perfect backdrops for grand entrances and lovely spots for silhouette photos.

- High-quality service should await you at most classic reception locations.

- Choose a color palette that harmonizes with the existing decor at your location of choice.

- Find out if other weddings will be taking place at your location on your wedding day so that schedules can be coordinated and overlaps avoided.

- If your guest list is large, look to a hotel ballroom. Most are ample in size, and many can accommodate hundreds of guests.

- Choose a site that is already ornately decorated, and you'll easily cut down on decor costs while wowing your guests.

- Love the look of a high vaulted ceiling? Looking to have a big dance band? Check with local musicians or your consultant for information about the acoustics in your venue. Ceilings can enhance or detract from sound quality.

service can be a blessing if you are too busy for vendor meetings and you're pleased with the professionals the location provides. With amenities like valet parking, coat check, and concierge assistance, you can expect your guests to feel well taken care of.

Other elegant event sites include castles, mansions, and historic buildings. After all, what could be more ideal for a fairy-tale wedding than a real castle or more appropriate for a vintage-inspired reception than a manor house with antique decor?

ZOOM

Private clubs provide similar amenities to hotels with the added bonus of additional privacy. Usually gated, and highly maintained, these locations have immaculately landscaped grounds and first-class service. If you are not a member of the club you're interested in, talk to the staff about finding someone to "sponsor" your reception.

Mansions and Historic Buildings

© photo by La Vie Photography

- Many historic locations are privately owned and have a personal feel that is unique from commercial venues.

- Pay attention to the traffic flow between entertainment spaces and ask the owners which areas, if any, are restricted from use.

- Services provided on site will vary in quality among locations. If you have your heart set on a particular caterer, florist, or cake designer, ask for permission for them to provide services.

Private Clubs and Golf Courses

© photo by J. Garner Photography

- Golf courses frequently restrict access to fairways, fountains, and other picturesque areas. Be sure you know what spaces are off-limits to you and your photographer.

- Private clubs range in size from enormous to petite and in usage requirements from ultra-exclusive to relaxed. Expect to find a wide range of options in your area.

- By hosting your wedding at a private club, you're giving your guests access to a location and service they couldn't experience otherwise.

CASUAL LOCATIONS

Homes, gardens, beaches, and country barns are natural locations for easy, elegant celebrations

Choosing to host a semiformal or casual affair allows you to create a playful, romantic ambiance that isn't available at more formal events and it gives you far more options for showing off your personal style.

If you, your parents, or other family members own a home with a stunning view, beautiful backyard, or special setting that can accommodate your guest list, what better place could there be to celebrate? Getting ready in your childhood bedroom or saying your vows under your favorite oak tree is an intimate way to bring back special memories and create many new ones.

Throughout the seasons, gorgeous garden spaces are

Private Homes

© photo by J. Garner Photography

- Treat a private home like any other off-site location when it comes to renting party supplies. Chances are you'll need tenting and the same number of rental tables, chairs, and other party items.

- If you have plenty of space for guests but don't have a big enough kitchen for your caterer, look for alternative spaces. Many caterers are experts at setting up kitchens in garages, tents, and other outbuildings.

Gardens and Parks

© photo by John and Joseph Photography

- A lovely garden provides natural decor, so you don't need elaborate floral arrangements or decorations, and photo ops like this one surround you.

- Visit your outdoor location at the same time of year that you're getting married so you'll know the type and color of flowers likely to be in bloom.

- Define an outdoor aisle using flower petals or lanterns. Aisle runners can be hard to keep tidy outside.

- Be sure to obtain the appropriate permits when renting a public location.

available for rent, from the manicured lawns and flower beds frequently found at privately owned estates, to the more natural environs of city parks. With Mother Nature doing the decorating, every backdrop is sure to be picture perfect.

Nothing says "kick back and relax" like a beach wedding. With sand between your toes and wind in your hair, you and your guests will be treated to the sound of the waves and the sun sparkling on the water. If you're an avid boater, surfer, scuba diver, or sun worshipper, the beach is a natural place for you to tie the knot. Destination beach weddings are all the rage these days, and resorts that specialize in beach ceremonies abound.

In regions where agriculture is an important element of community life, it's easy to find ranches and farms that have been converted to event spaces. If this uniquely romantic option appeals to you, consider going all out. Get a horse-drawn carriage to take you to your ceremony, follow it up with a delicious barbecue, and complete it with a bluegrass trio or country and western band.

Beaches

© photo by John and Joseph Photography

- Use natural landmarks like rock formations, overlooks, or trees to frame your ceremony location.

- Beaches are notoriously windy. Mix colored sand together in place of a unity candle and wear accessories that will easily stay in place.

- Consult an online weather resource to learn the weather patterns and tide tables on your wedding date.

- Give flip-flops, sunscreen, and lip balm to your guests as party favors.

Ranches and Country Farms

© photo by Positive Light Photography

- Play up an all-American theme with a ranch wedding on the weekend nearest July 4, and get married under the vast open sky.

- Take advantage of local farm-fresh foods by serving dishes made with in-season fruits and vegetables grown nearby.

- Use decorative hay bales. They make great places for people to sit for photos and if extra seating is needed during the ceremony.

- String simple twinkling lights and lanterns from rafters and trees for easy outdoor decor.

ALTERNATIVE LOCATIONS

Boats, wineries, museums, and other uncommon locations are perfect for one-of-a-kind events

Think outside of the box when it comes to finding a truly unique location for your ceremony or reception. Any place that appeals to you that can comfortably accommodate your guests can be considered. For maximum impact with minimal stress, be sure your location has hosted weddings before.

In areas like Seattle, San Diego, and Sarasota, tour boat companies abound, and it's easy to rent an entire boat or deck of a ship for your event and have the captain marry you while you're at it. From dinner and dancing on a sleek cruise ship to an intimate ceremony on a quaint old steamer, there is no better way to treat your guests to a stunning view while familiarizing them with their surroundings.

Tour Boats and Cruise Ships

© photo by GH Kim Photography

- Pick a beautifully crafted riverboat for a uniquely romantic ceremony and reception.

- Choose a sleek cruise ship with first-class service, entertainment, and amenities for a chic affair.

- Have plenty of cabin space to accommodate guests if it rains and plenty of room on deck for everyone to enjoy the breeze and watch the world go by.

- Weather at sea is unpredictable. Stick to inland waterways to ensure your guests' comfort, unless you're on an ocean liner.

Urban Spaces

© photo by John and Joseph Photography

- Every art gallery and museum has an artistic ambiance that can't be replicated anywhere else, and the topics showcased are endless.

- Industrial loft spaces match ultramodern styles and provide fun juxtapositions for romantic, casual affairs.

- Hip restaurants and clubs are prime spots to hold a second reception for your friends.

- Explore the neighborhood surrounding your venue. You may find some creative, alternative places for photo ops.

For artistic flair, look to museums, art galleries, lofts, and other urban places that offer event spaces for rent. Choose a place that you love to visit, like a history museum that showcases aeronautics or paleontology or an art museum that features modern or antique collections that you adore. Many museums have beautiful lighting, gorgeous decor, and plenty of parking.

Show off your region of the country by choosing an architectural or local landmark for your venue. Get married overlooking the Grand Canyon, Golden Gate Park, or the spot your city is best known for. Choose a picturesque winery to add real local flavor.

At locations from the snowcapped mountains of Switzerland to the sun-soaked beaches of French Polynesia, more and more couples are choosing to have destination weddings. By getting married in the same place that you're going for your honeymoon you offer guests an opportunity for an unforgettable vacation, plus you'll never have to say "Wish you were here!" to friends and family you want to celebrate with.

Local Landmarks and Wineries

© photo by GH Kim Photography

- Want to incorporate a favorite landmark into your day without getting married there? Ask your photographer to stop for photo ops on the way to your reception, like this couple did in front of Seattle's Space Needle.

- Did you meet at the playoffs? Then get married on home plate or have a family baseball game for your rehearsal dinner.

- Are you a wine enthusiast? Choose a winery for your location and give out wine with personalized labels as favors.

Destinations

© photo by John and Joseph Photography

- Choose a comfortable vacation spot that you've been fantasizing about. Book the ceremony and reception spaces right away and send your guests a save-the-date as early as possible.

- You'll need to be familiar with your destination, or hire a wedding planner who is, to plan your wedding without hassles.

- Incorporate the regional foods and themes associated with your location.

- Provide your guests with detailed travel and tourist information long before their arrival.

45

TENTS & COVERINGS

Shield yourself from the sun and rain with creative tenting and stylish umbrellas

Successfully incorporating the outdoors into your ceremony or reception requires some special considerations. You don't want rain, wind, or intense sun to ruin your otherwise perfect day, so you need a plan to deal with these potential obstacles.

To cover large groups of people, tents are the obvious choice and readily available in a variety of shapes and sizes.

Ranging in style from practical to posh, tents can simply offer protection from the elements or act as unique reception venues of their own. Tents are available through most large party and event rental companies and are often provided as an option by outdoor and view venues. Many sites offer gorgeous lighted tents as part of their wedding packages. Keep

Weatherproof Tenting

© photo by GH Kim Photography

- Call for several price quotes that include the tent, poles, and sidewalls you'll need, and ask about draping and decorative extras to make your tent beautiful.

- Wind, not rain, is the biggest weather challenge for tenting in many parts of the country. Ask your

rental company how much wind their tents can safely withstand.

- Choose a level space that drains easily during downpours and have a floor installed unless your foundation is completely flat and dry.

Decorative Tenting

© photo by Raj Tents

- To create a truly memorable outdoor event space, rent a tent made from beautifully draped fabrics for your ceremony, reception, or cocktail hour.

- Decorate the inside with chandeliers, oriental rugs, pillows, and comfortable

furniture to evoke an opulent Middle Eastern feel.

- Keep in mind that heating a tent's interior is fairly easy to do with space heaters or butane lanterns, but cooling it down with air-conditioning can be enormously expensive and loud.

46

in mind that if you plan to cover your guests for dining and dancing, you will need at least fifteen, if not eighteen, square feet per person, plus room for a dance floor and other extras. If your tent will be set up on anything other than a firm, dry foundation, you will also need to install subflooring to ensure your guests' safety and comfort, and lighting will be needed for practical as well as aesthetic reasons. Before renting your tent, check to see if you'll need a permit for setup and apply for it if necessary.

Other Considerations

© photo by GH Kim Photography

- Mark the size of the tent on the ground or on graph paper and be sure you can fit everything and everyone underneath it, so no one's left out in the cold!

- Supply your rental company with the number of guests attending, the size and quantity of tables and chairs, and the space required for the dance floor and catering areas.

- If your tent will require staking, contact your local gas and electric companies to obtain vital information about the location of underground lines.

Umbrellas and Parasols

© photo by John and Joseph Photography

- There's just something incredibly romantic about a couple huddled under an umbrella on their wedding day. Turn uninvited weather into a photo op by having stylish umbrellas on hand.

- Choose lacy umbrellas and vintage parasols to play up romantic, feminine fashions and solid coordinating colored umbrellas for a more modern look.

- Keep extra umbrellas by the exit doors of your ceremony and reception to make it easy for ushers to escort guests in the rain.

INVITATION BASICS

The right wording, style, and relevant information form the foundation for every invitation

When it comes to sending your wedding invitations, what you say and how you say it are important. An invitation acts as an informative guide for your guests, providing them with their first impression of your unique wedding style. You want to be sure that everyone receives basic information, including your names; the names of your hosts (traditionally your parents); the dates, times, and locations of both your ceremony and your reception; and an easy way to RSVP. Once those things are covered, there is no limit to the stylish options available for wedding invitations full of personality.

Order your invitations four to six months before your wedding and be ready to send them out six to eight weeks before

Invitation Style

© photo by Junebug Weddings

- Choose colors that complement your wedding color palette and designs that fit your style.

- Refer to your budget to determine if you'll be working with a custom invitation designer or ordering ready-made invitations. Both can be absolutely beautiful.

- Be sure you have confirmed your date and time with your ceremony and reception venues before you have your invitations printed.

- Send an invitation to yourself first to see how well it travels through the mail.

RSVP

© photo by Junebug Weddings

- Include an RSVP card and a self-addressed stamped envelope to make it easy for your guests to respond.

- Strict rules of etiquette require guests to promptly respond in writing to wedding invitations. Many people are not aware of this.

- Ask guests to respond by a certain date so there's no confusion.

- If you don't mind a phone call or e-mail response, add your phone number or e-mail address to your response card.

the event. For holiday weddings or weddings at the peak of the busy season, consider ordering them even sooner. Order plenty of extra invitations and envelopes to ensure that you're ready for inevitable mistakes and changes, and save a few for yourself and your family to use in albums and scrapbooks.

Choose papers, inks, fonts, specific wording, and design elements that show off your style and provide important clues as to the level of formality and type of attire expected.

············· GREEN ● LIGHT ·············

Reduce your carbon footprint and work with your invitation designer to cut down on the quantity of paper used in each invitation. The traditional layers of tissue and the multiple envelopes that used to be standard can easily be forgone in order to "go green" with your wedding invitations.

Addressing Your Guests

- Begin your invitation wording with the names of your hosts or your own names if you are hosting your wedding yourselves.

- Use wording that matches the formality of your event, but always adhere to basic rules of etiquette no matter how informal your wedding.

- Choose heavy papers, fine tissue liners, and formal fonts to announce an elegant black-tie affair and fun design elements like polka dots and bright colors to announce a wedding with a casual, informal feel.

Ecofriendly Options

- There's no need to sacrifice color with environmentally friendly soy-based inks. The clear, clean oil they're made from actually makes colors look brighter.

- Select tree-free papers made from cotton, linen, or bamboo for invitations that feel fantastic to the touch and are completely recyclable.

- Embrace the green movement by choosing a company dedicated to reducing its carbon footprint. Look for companies that recycle, cut down on waste, and belong to a carbon offsetting program.

SPREAD THE WORD

CLASSIC DESIGNS

Formal wording, classic paper, and traditional details combine to create a stylish, timeless message

Throughout most of the twentieth century, etiquette dictated that every couple's wedding invitations be designed essentially the same way. Printed on white paper with black ink or gold embossing powder, formal invitations included an inner and outer envelope, a reception card, an RSVP card, and traditional wording.

Preferred printing methods included the letterpress, with its old-fashioned movable type that furthers the handcrafted look, and the time-honored method of engraving, which still produces the most precise, elegant script available. Blind embossing (engraving without the ink) was often used to create lovely monograms, borders, and return addresses, and

Traditional Wording

© photo by Junebug Weddings

- The bride's parents are the traditional hosts of the wedding, and their names are spelled out first in the invitation.

- "Mr. and Mrs. Parents of the Bride request the honour of your presence" is the expected wording for church ceremonies.

- *Favour* and *honour* are the old English spellings used in traditional invitations.

- Addresses should be spelled out in full and there are no abbreviations used except for "Mr." and "Mrs."

Letterpress and Engraving

© photo by Junebug Weddings

- Today's letterpress invitations, like the one above, are often printed on cotton (tree-free) papers.

- Since the first printing of the Gutenberg Bible, the fine art of letterpress has been used to create one-of-a-kind invitations.

- Thermography has begun to replace engraving as the most popular method for printing classic invitations.

- Use fine tissues and vellum to add refinement and to act as a covering for engraved invitations to keep them from smudging.

calligraphy ruled the day as the popular way to address envelopes and create the handwritten look used by engravers.

Today's classic, formal invitations still incorporate these processes and follow the rules of etiquette in regard to proper wording, but choices of papers, inks, fonts, and embellishments are now personalized to offer you invitation options that are much more than what's commonly expected. By incorporating traditional designs with modern details you're free to create a uniquely sophisticated statement.

Chic and Sophisticated

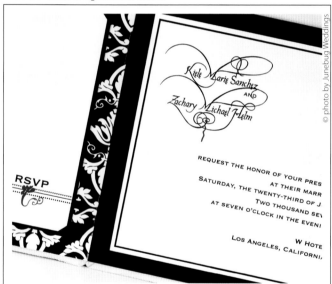

© photo by Junebug Weddings

- Black-and-white is still the color combination most associated with the invitations of chic, formal affairs.

- Strong colors like red, bronze, and gold accentuate classic black-and-white designs.

- Mounting your invitation on a bifold or trifold mat so it can be easily displayed highlights the important nature of your event.

- Artistic embellishments like your choice of modern fonts or decorative motifs and borders help you show off your sophisticated style.

Romantic and Timeless

© photo by Junebug Weddings

- Classic swirls, floral details, and other organic and nature-inspired embellishments lend romance to your invitation design.

- Feminine, handwritten typefaces and calligraphy take the romance even further and will never look dated.

- Soft colors like powder pink, apricot, taupe, and dove blue look lovely and add a delicate touch to creamy off-white papers.

- Vintage-inspired fonts and embellishments are timeless additions that add a feeling of quality and easy elegance.

CASUAL DESIGNS
Simplified wording and carefree details set a tone of easy elegance

Casually designed invitations give you the freedom to veer off the ultratraditional track to get creative and express more of your personal wedding style. Formal wording can be softened, papers and colors can come from a broader artistic palette, graphics and patterns can add fun and excitement, and natural accents can be used to show off the theme of your event.

Even when using casual wording for your invitations, it's always smart to stay respectful and gracious. Be sure you're acknowledging those hosting your event and warmly welcoming those being invited. Whether your invitations say something simple like, "Together with their parents, Kimberly Elizabeth Loewen and Adam Curtis Bamberg invite you to share in the joy of their wedding day," or "Joyously, gleefully,

Casual Wording

© photo by Junebug Weddings

- Instead of the classic wording like "request the honour of your presence," you can say something more casual-sounding, like "invite you to share in the joy of their wedding day."

- You can include your parents' names in the host line, whether or not they are the event's main financial contributors, or simply say "together with their families."

- Get even more playful with your wording if it matches the tone and theme of your event.

Paper Textures and Colors

© photo by Junebug Weddings

- Handmade papers, with their slightly irregular surfaces, are pretty and feminine with a homemade feel.

- Modern-style invitations can benefit from papers with ribbing, strong angular textures, or lush metallic finishes.

- Casual invitations can use color combinations not traditionally considered bridal. Go bold with intensely colored papers, inks, and strong contrasts.

- Have fun experimenting with color; you may be surprised at the combinations you love most!

giddily, and ecstatically, we invite you to celebrate as Kim and Adam tie the knot," choose your words carefully and with reverence for those helping you.

Bold colors and detailed paper textures can add depth and personality that classic white card stock simply can't touch. Look at samples, visit stationery stores, and find examples of designs you love for the best and most useful inspiration.

Patterns and graphics offer an even further addition of creative expression, and there are unending possibilities to choose from. Do you and your partner gravitate toward abstract patterns or realistic imagery, feminine flourishes, or angular geometry? Narrow it down to your favorite themes and work with your designer to come up with the perfect look, or play with unusual combinations that creatively represent you both.

Organic accents inspired by the natural world work wonders to communicate your wedding theme. You can incorporate colors or imagery inspired by Mother Nature, ecofriendly materials, or an authentic bit of nature itself to convey the style of your event.

Graphics and Patterns

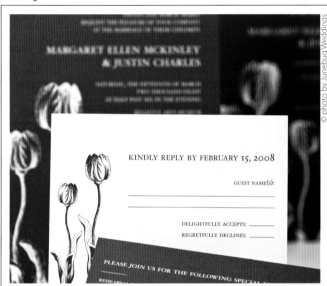

© photo by Junebug Weddings

- Use graphics that represent your specific wedding details. Choose flowers you'll be using in your wedding decor, a pattern that will carry through to your table settings, or decorative accents present in the architecture of your venue.

- Find inspiration for invitation graphics in your wedding dress or other wedding day fashions.

- Balance the masculine and feminine in your invitation graphics so that you'll both love the look. Try one's chosen pattern in the other's favorite color, or vice versa.

Natural Accents

© photo by Junebug Weddings

- Tie a beautifully pressed golden leaf to the front cover of your fall wedding invitation, or use a small twig as a closure to radiate the fresh new feeling of spring.

- Actual organic details incorporated into your invitation design can be powerful and unique design elements.

- Organic graphics and patterns can evoke the season you're getting married in: tulips for spring, poppies for summer, leaves for fall, and holly for winter.

ALTERNATIVE DESIGNS
Let your imagination take flight to create a one-of-a-kind invitation

If great design is a true love of yours, then go all the way with your invitations and choose an alternative size, unusual structure, or high-tech format to make them truly one of a kind.

Paper can be ordered in numerous shapes and sizes of ready-made pocket folders and enclosures. Pocket folders allow for extra pages to be included inside and can open either horizontally like a book, vertically like an envelope, or from the center outward in all directions. Take a look at your local paper store or online to see the variety of options and do-it-yourself kits available.

If you or your fiancé work in the tech industry or are right at home with your computer and electronic gadgets, consider using CDs, DVDs, digital images, or Web sites to add fun to your wedding invitations.

Paper Enclosures

© photo by Junebug Weddings

- Gatefold invitations, like the one shown above, have three panels, while single folios have just two.

- A booklet-style invitation is like a mini album, with multiple pages available to communicate lots of useful information.

- Blossom- or star-style envelopments have a base that holds your invitation card and flaps on each edge that fold closed toward the center.

- Paper invitations can be mailed nestled inside flat gift boxes and surrounded with decorative papers or treats.

High Tech

© photo by Junebug Weddings

- This CD of love songs was sent to guests to get everyone caught up in the romance before they arrived at the wedding.

- Invitations in the form of a DVD can match a cinematic-themed wedding or act like a high-tech Web site, informing guests of your favorite restaurants, clubs, and places to visit to help travelers feel more at home.

- Include a DVD slide show of images of you, your partner, and your family and friends.

The tiniest details can add up to create a truly one-of-a-kind invitation design. Once you get your basic design ideas down, think about ways to expand the concept to every piece of your wedding paper ensemble.

Destination-themed weddings offer the perfect inspiration for creative invitations. Pull graphics, colors, and cultural details from the travel industry or the country to which you're headed to create invitations with a spirit of adventure.

One of a Kind

- You can create postage stamps with your own photo or graphic for an ultrapersonalized touch. See the Resources section for sources.

- Every piece of your invitation suite can have unique design elements. The envelope, RSVP card, return envelope, and reception card can all have different but complementary details printed on them.

- Many invitation designers can adapt one of their existing designs with personalized elements just for you.

Destination Theme

- For international travel, create a booklet invitation that looks like a realistic passport.

- Airline boarding passes make for fun and familiar designs for destination save-the-dates, wedding invitations, or seating cards.

- Include an elegant map in your invitation for destination weddings or for out-of-town guests. Have one custom illustrated with your wedding venues and other points of interest highlighted, or find a charming old-fashioned reproduction that will lend an air of history to the trip.

SPREAD THE WORD

INFORMATIVE EXTRAS
Both print and online options keep your guests informed

Tying together your invitation wardrobe has never been easier. From one-of-a-kind save-the-dates to matching programs, gifts, menus, and favors, there is a host of unique ways to finish your statement and keep your guests informed.

If you're planning on inviting guests who will need to travel to your wedding and make arrangements months in advance, then a stylish save-the-date card sent four to six months before your wedding is a thoughtful way to let them know how much their presence will mean to you.

Once your big day dawns, those attending your wedding will appreciate a detailed program that helps them prepare for the specifics of your ceremony. When you've tied the knot and it's time to enjoy your reception, seating cards act to direct guests to their places, where they're likely to find

Save-the-Dates

© photo by Junebug Weddings

- Whether they're custom designed or DIY, designing a save-the-date is a fun way to start planning your wedding together.

- Choose colors and styles that complement your main invitation. This will set a cohesive tone right from the beginning.

- Keep in mind the time of year and location when sending your save-the-date cards. Remember that traveling on holidays to popular destinations can be problematic.

- Include lodging and travel information if you have special tips to share.

Ceremony Extras

© photo by Junebug Weddings

- Besides letting guests know how your ceremony will unfold, programs give them something to read while they wait for you to come down the aisle.

- Include the names of your wedding party and how they are affiliated with you

- to help familiarize guests from different parts of your life.

- Sweet extras like the story of how you first met or when you first knew you were in love let your guests in on what makes your relationship unique.

people they will connect with. Simple tabletop accents like creative wedding favors, trivia questions about the two of you, or stories about your courtship will entertain your guests and break the ice with friends and family who are still getting to know one another.

For an easy way to communicate with guests from across the globe, consider building a personal wedding Web site. Include directions, RSVP options, lodging information, and local attractions for out-of-town guests.

Reception Extras

© photo by Junebug Weddings

- Printed menus let guests know what to look forward to and alert them to anything that may not be on their list of approved foods.

- Table cards typically identify tables by name or number; try using place names like London or Paris

for a chic urban event or names of artists for a reception held at a museum or art gallery.

- Recipe cards given as favors that offer dishes or drinks from your family or favorite restaurant will be used again and passed on.

Your Wedding Web Site

© photo by Junebug Weddings

- It's considered improper to include registry information on your wedding invitation, but listing it on your wedding Web site is perfectly acceptable.

- Many sites allow you to have photo galleries, which can be great for introducing your family members and

members of your wedding party to your guests who may not know everyone.

- If you've designed a simple ecofriendly wedding invitation, you can direct guests to view your wedding Web site to get all the additional information they will need.

SPREAD THE WORD

59

YOU'RE THE BRIDE!

Bridal tips for what to do when every decision is up to you

It used to be that a woman had very little to do when it came to planning her own wedding. Her mother would make the arrangements, her parents would invite all of the guests, and the groom did his best to arrive on time. The bride was responsible for buying her husband's wedding band, providing gifts for the members of her bridal party, setting up beauty appointments, and sending out thank-you notes. As a modern bride you'll do all of that and more. Chances are you'll be involved in almost every decision, from deciding on your wedding date to the flavors in your cake. Your to-do list can quickly become overwhelming.

That's why it's important to set up a support team of professionals, friends, and family members who can help make your wedding planning fun and easy. You'll want to delegate

The Modern Bride

© photo by GH Kim Photography

- Traditionally brides have been responsible for sending thank-you notes; nowadays your groom needs to get in on the act as well.

- Include his ring, your bridal party gifts, and your personal stationery in your own budget if your parents are hosting your wedding.

- "To your own self be true." Don't let fantasies or false expectations take over when planning your real wedding.

- You absolutely can't please everyone, so just remember to be gracious and recognize good intentions.

Your Support Team

© photo by La Vie Photography

- People's schedules and talents differ. Don't expect help, just ask for it nicely and always say thank you.

- Offer members of your bridal party fun things to do like help you pick out your dress or brainstorm DIY opportunities.

- Whenever people help you, let them know how much you appreciate them right away. They'll be much more likely to pitch in the next time you ask.

- Draw on the hobbies and passions of others when delegating responsibility.

early and often to people who want to help. Your mom and members of your bridal party are the obvious first choices to turn to. If you're hiring a wedding consultant, he or she will be a valuable asset in helping you create a stylish ceremony and reception that runs smoothly. If you aren't hiring a planner, you'll need to look to family members, friends, and other trusted resources to ensure you have the support you need.

Don't be shy about asking for recommendations and references. Experienced wedding vendors should have numerous current references to give to you, and newlyweds love to talk about what worked and didn't work at their own weddings. Listen to advice gracefully and thank the person giving it, but don't feel pressured to follow every recommendation to a T—and don't give the impression that you will follow it unless you're planning to.

Follow your instincts about what you need to stay healthy, happy, and organized so you can thoroughly enjoy this exciting time!

Helpful Advice

© photo by John and Joseph Photography

- If you choose to tackle your own planning, just stay meticulously organized. Create a calendar in your PDA or online and post another one where you can't miss it. Celebrate your milestones!

- Contrary to popular belief, wedding consultants can save you both time and money, in addition to making your wedding stress free.

- Consider setting up a "wedding office" in your home or at your parents' home and keep everything in one place.

Trusted Referrals

© photo by GH Kim Photography

- There's no one like someone who has been through it to lend her support. Connect with other brides at work and online.

- Once you've decided with whom you want to work, relax and trust them to do their job. Communicate openly and be direct with your desires.

- No matter what happens, keep a sense of humor. It's your attitude that determines if a problem is a minor setback or a major disaster.

SOMETHING OLD, SOMETHING NEW

Bring a little magic to your big day with these traditional good luck charms

The Victorian-era English saying "Something old, something new, something borrowed, something blue, and a silver sixpence in your shoe" is a good luck tradition that many of today's brides still follow. Each part of the poem has significance, and interpreting it your own way can add sweetness, creativity, and a little extra magic to your day.

"Something old" signifies a connection to the past, including your family values and family history. You may want to wear a piece of heirloom jewelry or your mother's wedding veil as a sign of this bond, or you may choose to incorporate into your ceremony a favorite photo, childhood story, or song that has sentimental value to you and your family members.

Something Old

© photo by J. Garner Photography

- Make your getaway in a vintage Rolls Royce or hold your reception at a beautiful historic site.

- Look to your mom, his mom, and your grandmothers for lovely jewelry and accessories that have family significance.

- Carry a picture from your parents' wedding or a love letter from your father to your mother in your purse.

- Wear your mother's wedding dress or veil, or carry a purse or compact mirror she used on her wedding day.

Something New

© photo by John and Joseph Photography

- Wear new shoes, choose a new perfume, or buy a new shade of lipstick.

- Have a new cocktail recipe invented and named after you and your partner. Serve it at your reception with a recipe-card coaster.

- Buy new earrings or a charm for your charm bracelet that can be passed down to future generations.

- Ask your guests to bring a wish or a small token to add to your "time capsule box" to be opened on your silver wedding anniversary.

"Something new" indicates hope and an optimistic look at the road ahead. This can be represented by any new item you purchase or be a gesture of what you hope for the future. Maybe you would like to start your own new tradition? Think of new and creative ways to honor your friends or support your favorite cause.

"Something borrowed" denotes the respect you have for others who have been role models in your life. Choose to borrow something of significance from someone who exemplifies the traits of a good partner and let a little of their wisdom "rub off" on you.

"Something blue" is a sign of fidelity and true love. For many years before the white wedding dress came into vogue, brides were married in blue as a symbol of their purity. Nowadays brides wear just a touch of blue to finish the charm, often incorporating the color into their garters, shoes, lingerie, or wedding bouquet. No matter what you choose to do, make it fun and make it meaningful.

Something Borrowed

© photo by J. Garner Photography

- Borrow a special item to wear from one of your closest friends and ask her to help you put it on.

- Borrow a passage, song, or special prayer from the wedding ceremony of a couple you admire.

- Get married at the home of a relative or spend your honeymoon at a family member's vacation property or time-share.

- Use a pearl-handled knife or decorative cake cutter that you've borrowed from a friend, or put your parents' cake topper on top of your cake.

Something Blue

© photo by John and Joseph Photography

- Tie a light blue ribbon around your garter or have one woven into the handle of your bouquet.

- Incorporate forget-me-nots, larkspur, delphinium, or love-in-a-mist blossoms into your bridal bouquet for a romantic touch of blue.

- Buy yourself some lacy blue underthings or other fun blue accessories.

- Have your cake decorated with blueberries and other fresh fruits and flowers, or serve blueberry pies and tarts as an alternative to your wedding cake.

TIME-HONORED TRADITIONS

Sentimental touches and good luck symbols add romance to your wedding

You probably don't want it to rain on your wedding day, but if it does, don't worry. It's considered to be good luck! Whether or not you believe in magic or miracles, incorporating some sweet and sentimental folklore into your wedding day can make you feel extra lucky, and what could be wrong with that? There are lots of ways to add some new twists to old traditions.

Light a unity candle to commemorate the joining together of your two lives and two families. This is a tradition used by cultures throughout the world. Have your moms light the first two candles. You can also fashion a unity bouquet by having each parent bring a flower to the altar to create a special floral display.

Good Luck Symbols

© photo by La Vie Photography

- Rain on your wedding day is actually good luck, so make the most of it with fun photo opportunities using umbrellas and parasols.

- The month of June, named after Juno, the Roman goddess of hearth and home, has long been the lucky month for marriages.

- Make your own good luck. Instead of a guest book, have your guests sign note cards with special wishes for your life together. Put them in a box and read them on your anniversary.

Expressions of Unity

© photo by La Vie Photography

- Unity candles are perfect for indoor ceremonies, and unity bouquets are perfect for outside ceremonies where wind can be a factor.

- Exchange flower leis with each other and present them to your parents as a lovely symbol of unity.

- Have your flower girl or ring bearer ring a silver bell during your recessional. Take the bell home and ring it to call your family together for holiday meals.

- Pour different colors of sand into a vase to symbolize the joining of your families.

Have all the ladies who are close to you sign the bottom of your shoes; you'll be carried along throughout your big day by their love, and the one whose name disappears first will have extra good luck for a year.

Instead of asking your guests if anyone needs to "speak now or forever hold their peace," have your guests say "We will" when asked, "Who will support this couple?" Ask the married couples attending to renew their vows silently as you exchange yours.

Sentimental Touches

© photo by La Vie Photography

- A silver sixpence in your shoe is a part of the "something old" tradition. Buy a real sixpence online or use a shiny new penny.

- The sixpence tradition dates back to medieval Scotland, where the groom placed a silver coin in his shoe for good luck.

- Share some sweetness by placing a small drop of honey on each other's lips before you kiss.

- Have your guests introduce themselves to one another by saying, "Peace be with you," or another positive greeting.

Your First Look

© photo by J. Garner Photography

- Even if you've lived together for years, you may not want to be seen until you come down the aisle. Do what you think is most romantic.

- Give your dad a hug when he gives you away. It's a big moment for him, too.

- Are you seeing each other before your ceremony? Make the first time he sees you in your dress special. Select a quiet place for him to wait, then surprise him with how beautiful you look.

GOING TO THE CHAPEL

Walk down the aisle with confidence with these wedding tips for every step along the way

You'll want to wake up feeling refreshed on your wedding day, ready to get gorgeous and enjoy every moment. Don't jump out of bed; remember to breathe deep and let the joy of the day fill your heart. Enjoy a cup of coffee or tea with your girls and discuss any last-minute details before you become "the bride."

Today is not the time for a bad hair day, so have your hair and makeup done first, providing plenty of time to make any desired changes. Be sure you have a copy of your vows, the "survival kit" discussed on page 94–95, and any touch-up makeup you may need with you. Change the message on your cell phone to announce that it's your wedding day and

Celebrate from the Start

© photo by Yours by John Photography

- Gather the women you want with you to witness your transformation into a bride.

- Resist the urge to stay up late celebrating the night before your wedding. You'll need eight hours of sleep for the day ahead.

- Have a healthy breakfast and drink plenty of water.

- Designate one area of your getting-ready room for your bridal party to put their belongings. Almost every moment is a photo op, so you'll want things neat and tidy.

Get Gorgeous

© photo by John and Joseph Photography

- Schedule plenty of time to get ready so you can enjoy the process of seeing yourself becoming a bride.

- Be sure your photographer is ready to capture it all, from your last-minute makeup touches to buttoning up your dress.

- Bring an extra pair of shoes with you in case your feet need relief.

- If you're wearing colored polish on your fingers or toes, have an extra bottle on hand just in case a major chip or broken nail occurs.

direct people to call your maid of honor or another designated member of your bridal party.

Arrive at your ceremony location with plenty of time to have any prewedding photos taken, and give yourself at least thirty minutes to relax somewhere outside of view of your wedding guests as they arrive.

Remember to pause as you begin to make your way down the aisle and proceed slowly, taking in the faces of your loved ones and most important, your groom waiting at the altar. Don't worry about the ceremony itself; your officiant will do most of the talking, and if you should make a mistake, you'll never have a more supportive group of people to share it with. When it comes time for the kiss, keep in mind that your photographer needs to catch it, so savor it! Then, when your officiant announces that you're married, smile big and once again take your time coming down the aisle so your photographer has plenty of time to capture your grand exit.

Get Married

© photo by John and Joseph Photography

- Prior to your ceremony, ask your officiant to stand to one side during the kiss. That way it's just the two of you newlyweds who will stand out in your photos.

- If your dress is going to wrinkle, you may want to put it on at your ceremony location.

- Carry a pretty hanky with you even if you usually don't cry; you may surprise yourself.

- Remember to breathe, and don't lock your knees.

Exit in Style

© photo by La Vie Photography

- Take some time alone immediately after your ceremony to connect with each other and let your guests gather for your exit to the reception.

- Ask your planner or photographer to assemble guests in two rows leading to your getaway car.

- You have up to forty-five minutes for pictures after your ceremony. If you're having them taken at a park or viewpoint, choose a location close to your event so unexpected traffic doesn't throw off your timing.

RECEPTION EVENTS

It's your celebration; enjoy every moment, from your first dance to your final exit

Your grand entrance into your reception venue is a delightful moment for everyone. Create anticipation without causing impatience by arriving thirty to forty-five minutes after the party has begun. Your DJ or MC should get everyone's undivided attention and announce your arrival with flair.

When it comes to your first dance, don't let nerves get in the way. It's not a professional dance competition, so if you're shy, just relax and dance within your comfort zone. However, if you're a true dance diva and can't wait to get out on the floor, feel free to show off; your guests will love it!

After your first dance together, it's expected that the next man who gets a chance is your father. If that isn't possible,

Your Grand Entrance

© photo by GH Kim Photography

- Take time out to freshen up before you join your party. With so many people excited to see you, you may have trouble getting away later on.

- Including your bridal party in the announcement is a fun way to introduce them to your guests.

- Your entrance is the perfect time to thank guests for coming and invite them to enjoy themselves. If you're not having a receiving line, mention that you'll be coming to each table to say hello.

Your First Dance

© photo by La Vie Photography

- A few dance lessons can do a world of wonders for your confidence and be a fun way to spend time together.

- Practice your moves several times before your big night so you can concentrate on being in the moment, not on getting the steps right.

- Choose a song with special meaning that you'll both love to dance to in the years ahead.

- Get creative! Tango, rumba, or waltz your way through this special reception tradition.

you can choose someone who has acted as a father figure in your life, your best man, your best male friend, or all of them in succession. It's amazing how much this special gesture can mean to the ones you love.

Cutting your cake will signal an early departure opportunity for guests with tired children and other considerations, so cut it after your first dance and before your party really picks up steam; that way your friends will have a chance to say good-bye.

YELLOW LIGHT

If your guest list includes lots of single women, the bouquet toss is a fun event. But if most of your friends are married, it can be an anticlimactic moment. As an alternative consider giving your bouquet to your mother or mother-in-law as a sign of your love and respect.

Cake Cutting

© photo by La Vie Photography

- Start by cutting a small piece from the bottom tier of your cake, then place it on a plate and use two forks to share a single bite.

- Save the top tier to freeze and share on your anniversary or other special occasion.

- Remember that sharing cake is a sign of sharing sweetness. So don't smash the cake in each other's faces; that's no way to start your marriage or keep your dress clean.

Bouquet Toss

© photo by John and Joseph Photography

- If you would like to save your bouquet as a keepsake, have two made: one to toss and one to keep.

- The same is true of your garter; get an extra one to toss away if you'll be following this tradition.

- Little girls just love the bouquet toss, but you don't want them to get knocked down in the excitement. Have little ones stand to the side, then throw to the center.

THANK-YOU NOTES

Show your love and appreciation with creative notes and thoughtful gifts

To celebrate your marriage, your friends and family will shower you with their good intentions. They'll give you presents, throw parties in your honor, and share their time and talents with you. To show your gratitude, you'll want to share your thanks with them in ways that will touch their hearts.

Start by sending a handwritten thank-you note to each and every person who gives you something of value. Mention the giver's gift or contribution and why you appreciate it. While handwritten notes may be rare these days, they are still a necessary part of wedding etiquette, and sending them is something you shouldn't overlook. Try to send them out within three weeks of receiving gifts, and don't procrastinate.

Thank-You Cards

© photo by Junebug Weddings

- Order your thank-you notes with your invitations and other printed items; you may get a price break from your printer.

- Every gift giver puts careful thought into his or her gift. Be just as thoughtful with your reply.

- Thank-you notes are the last impression that guests will have of your wedding. Their importance cannot be overemphasized.

- Don't listen to people who say you have up to a year to reply; three months is the maximum time allowed.

Handwritten Notes

© photo by John and Joseph Photography

- Don't worry if your handwriting is less than perfect. As long as it's legible, it's the effort that counts.

- Hand address your envelopes and your cards. Preprinted labels and messages are an etiquette no-no.

- Should you receive a gift that's not quite your cup of tea, don't rave on about how much you love it. Just say "Thank you for the (fill in the blank). I'll think of you whenever I use it."

For people who go the extra mile to show their support, look for thoughtful gifts and creative ways to say thanks. Did your favorite cousin give you the china pattern that you wanted? Then have him over for dinner to enjoy it. Did your sister walk the aisles of every local wedding show with you without complaining? Then treat her to a day at the spa to give her a chance to put her feet up. However you choose to express your appreciation, be thoughtful and authentic.

MAKE IT EASY

Keep an ongoing gratitude list and schedule time at least twice a month to write and send out your thank-you notes together. Have fun with this important obligation by setting up special cocktails, drinks, or snacks or listening to your favorite music.

Thoughtful Gifts

© photo by La Vie Photography

- Bake some cookies or make a cake for a person who gave you nice things for your kitchen.

- Send perennial flower bulbs to a gardening enthusiast for a lovely gift that will be appreciated year after year.

- Start an annual "girl's night out," and celebrate with your bridal party every year the night before your anniversary.

- Send a wedding photo that includes the recipient as a follow-up to your thank-you card.

Your Gratitude List

© photo by GH Kim Photography

- Make it a habit to celebrate the reasons that you're grateful for each other. It's a sweet and touching way to connect and a great habit to begin together now.

- Don't forget to make a record of all the gifts you receive and who gave them.

With all that's going on it's easy to forget which gift came from which person.

- Resist any temptation to take your thank-you notes with you on your honeymoon. There will be time to send them when you get back.

TRADITIONAL RESPONSIBILITIES

Your important role as the groom—from the proposal to your honeymoon

You've popped the big question and gotten the yes you were looking for. Now your journey to the altar has begun. If you've already read Chapters 1 and 2, you've got a good idea of what's most important to you and your fiancée; you know what you can afford and who you're going to invite and you're ready to take the plunge into planning.

First, get organized. Approach your wedding like a project manager. If you haven't already, create a spreadsheet with all of your contacts and budget information and make your big to-do list. Once that's done, choose your best man and your bridal party based on friendship, family ties, and common sense. You want someone who is organized, reliable, and

You're a Lucky Man!

© photo by GH Kim Photography

- Consider writing an engagement announcement that fits your wedding style. A message from you about what a lucky man you are signals your involvement and gratitude for having found the woman of your dreams.

- Ask her how you can be the most help to her. A little support can go a long way.

- Write and mail your own thank-you cards, and don't forget to include one to her parents for raising the love of your life.

Set Up Your Support Team

© photo by Barbie Hull Photography

- Your best man will have a lot of duties before and during your wedding. In addition to choosing someone reliable, be sure he has the time and energy for the job.

- If you're having a hard time choosing between your best friend and your brother, etiquette says family first.

- Cousins and close friends make fantastic groomsmen and ushers.

- Your ring bearer should be at least four years old and your altar boys at least ten to avoid mishaps.

excited to help as your best man, and guys you can count on in a pinch for your groomsmen. Communicate to your guys what part you want them to play in your big day, and coordinate your wedding party fashion with your fiancée's. You'll get lots of tips on how dress to impress in the pages ahead.

Once the basics are covered, plan your honeymoon and book your wedding-night room ASAP. Research diligently and get an early jump on the best travel arrangements and the most romantic accommodations. A stellar honeymoon will bring you big husband points and great memories.

Add buying your wedding bands, creating your song list, and getting your marriage license to the list of things you'll need to do together. You'll probably be on your own when it comes to buying gifts, writing your toasts and vows, and arranging for transportation. Start setting up appointments to interview potential vendors, and don't forget to check with your fiancée to find out about other appointments she would like you to make or attend with her.

Start Planning Your Honeymoon

© photo by Yours by John Photography

- Check all of your reservations, including transportation to and from your accommodations, twice.

- Don't be fooled by ads and photos. Ask lots of questions, get referrals, and find out if any events or construction may affect your visit.

- If you're traveling out of the country, arrange for all travel requirements for passports, blood tests, and immunizations before you book.

- Have dinner reservations ready for the first night that you arrive.

Buy Gifts and Finalize Details

© photo by La Vie Photography

- Shop for gifts well in advance, and help your fiancée register for the wedding gifts you'll be receiving from guests.

- Make a list of everyone you want to thank at your reception, and don't forget to include your wife in your list.

- Research your state's marriage requirements online many months before your wedding date.

- Don't hesitate to verify your agreements by requesting written confirmations. Keep all of your receipts in the same place for easy access.

GET CREATIVE
Show off your personality with little details that make a big statement

More and more men are finding that wedding planning becomes a lot of fun by bringing their great ideas and personalities to the table. If you would like to get more involved, then by all means jump in and get creative!

Use your top ten priority list to help inspire you. Did you prioritize great music and dancing? Then hire the DJ or band for your reception. Create a playlist full of favorites from your dating years together and songs that bring back memories for your family and friends, or pick a fabulous band to bring your party to life. Give out CDs of your music mix as a reception favor.

Take charge of the bar. Put together a drink list that your

Play Your Song

© photo by La Vie Photography

- Your first dance is the most important song of the night, so be sure your fiancée is as thrilled with it as you are.

- Suggest taking dance lessons as a date idea. You'll be glad you did when all eyes are on you.

- A DJ can make or break a party, so be sure yours has plenty of experience.

- Let your DJ or band leader know your likes and dislikes. You don't want to be doing the Macarena by surprise.

Take Charge of the Bar

J & B
Brooke : Justin
RED WINE 8 17 07

© photo by Positive Light Photography

- Order your own signature wine from a local vineyard. Have a label made like the one shown above, from an engagement photo or motif from your wedding invitation.

- Remember the kids. Have grenadine on hand for Shirley Temples or serve ice-cream floats. Buy crazy straws to make them smile.

- Bar tabs can really add up. If your budget doesn't allow for an open bar with cocktails, stick to beer and wine or other beverages. No-host bars and weddings don't mix well.

guests will appreciate, from your buddy's favorite beer to your grandma's favorite lemonade. Get a signature cocktail made for the two of you and keep the recipe for your anniversaries.

To make a great impression both coming and going, arrange for unique wedding transportation that fits you to a T. Arrive in a golf cart or take off in a tugboat, show up in a Mini Cooper or wave good-bye from the back of a classic limousine. Great rides make for great photo ops.

Arrive in Style

© photo by J. Garner Photography

- European sports cars and classic American convertibles are perfect for casual weddings.

- Antique motorcars and stretch limousines add an elegant touch to formal affairs.

- Horse-drawn carriages, motorcycles, bicycles, boats, and trolleys make fun alternative transportation.

- If you'll be using your own car, chances are someone will decorate it. Be sure your best man knows that shaving cream eats paint but window paint found at party-supply stores doesn't.

Special Surprises

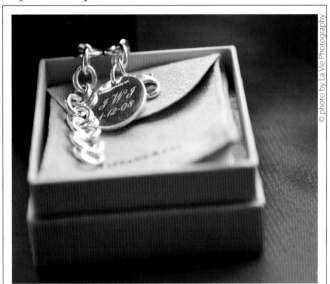

© photo by La Vie Photography

- The traditional wedding day gift for your bride is a piece of jewelry she can keep and cherish forever.

- Ask your best man to check in with your bride the morning of your wedding. Have him deliver her a gift, a poem, or a note from you about how much you love her.

- Plan a reception surprise you know she'll love, like fireworks, a silly song written by your friends, or a video of the two of you from your childhoods to the present.

TUXEDOS & SUITS

Formal, casual, or in between, suits and tuxes make for a modern and stylish wedding day look

Everyone loves a man in a suit, and your wedding day gives you the opportunity to put together a truly spectacular formal look to woo your bride, wow your guests, and make you feel like a million dollars. There are many options available for men's formal wear, from the most formal white-tie tuxedo to the most casual linen suit, so consider your event's theme, location, time of day, and time of year to find the perfect look for you.

White-tie is considered the most formal classification of menswear and brings an aura of history and glamour to your event. Unlike other styles of menswear, where you can be a little creative with your choices, white-tie is extremely

White-Tie

© photo by John and Joseph Photography

- The white-tie tailcoat has a horizontal, cutaway front that leaves long tails in the back. It looks double breasted, but it doesn't actually fasten in the front.

- The white bow tie and waistcoat are made of matching materials, typically cotton pique.

- The daytime version of white-tie is called morning dress. The most noticeable difference is the cut and color of the coat and the use of a necktie or cravat.

Black-Tie

© photo by GH Kim Photography

- Traditional collar options on a tuxedo range from the long rounded shawl collar and the sleek and elegant notch lapel (as shown above) to the more dramatic and angular peak lapel.

- Bow ties and formal neckties should match the fabric of your tux lapels.

- If you wear a cummerbund, its pleats should face up.

- The daytime equivalent of black-tie is called the stroller and is very similar to morning dress, except that a necktie is nearly always worn and the coat has no tails.

traditional and the guidelines of what is appropriate are very specific. Worn only after 6:00 in the evening, white-tie consists of a black tailcoat, black trousers worn with suspenders, a white winged-collar shirt, a white waistcoat, and a white bow tie.

Black-tie is the most common level of formal wear. It consists of a classic black tuxedo or a modern variation. In the summer months or in very warm climates, a white dinner jacket can be worn with a simple black cummerbund and bow tie, reminiscent of James Bond or Humphrey Bogart in *Casablanca*.

Both formal and casual suits are very popular for modern grooms and their wedding parties, as they are still appropriate for this kind of special occasion but leave a little more room for alternative style. Most tuxedos and formal suits are available to rent, but a purchased one that's tailored to fit you will be the best quality. If you think you'll have the opportunity to wear it three or four times a year, or if you want it as a special memento of your day, consider buying instead of renting.

Formal Suits

© photo by GH Kim Photography

- These men are wearing black suits, which creates a formal and cohesive look.

- Single-breasted suits usually have two or three buttons. Two-button jackets have a longer vertical shape and flatter most body types. Three-button jackets have a broader shape and look best on large or tall men.

- Suits are made from wools that are categorized by numbers like Super 110, 120, or 150. Generally the higher the number, the finer and softer the wool.

Casual Suits

© photo by Yours by John Photography

- Navy and tan suits look more casual than their black or dark gray counterparts.

- In a well-fitting suit, your shirtsleeves should extend about half an inch beyond your jacket cuff and your shirt collar about half an inch above your jacket collar.

- Light-colored linen, poplin, and seersucker suits are cool, comfortable, and casual during warm summertime weddings.

- A suit worn without a tie or with a sweater vest underneath is a fun informal menswear option.

ALTERNATIVE ATTIRE

Fun and fashionable menswear alternatives can show off your personality and unique personal style

If your wedding theme has a personal twist, why not let your wedding fashion reflect the mood of the day? Lighten up the fashion rules for your wedding day and wear a creative alternative option that perfectly matches your style, your wedding theme, or your environment.

Mix-and-match suits offer a sharp, semiformal look but allow for a more unique interpretation. Combine different colored pants and jackets, go jacket free, or play with the colors and patterns of your shirt, tie, or other accessories.

For a casual wedding on a warm beach or near the sand, a heavy wool suit obviously just won't do. Adopt the laid-back feeling of a tropical vacation and incorporate breezy fabrics

Alternative Suits

© photo by John and Joseph Photography

- A nicely tailored neutral-colored suit looks great paired with your favorite colors. Play up your wedding color palette or the color of your eyes. Experiment with a patterned or boldly hued tie like the one shown above.

- Wearing tan slacks with a navy blue blazer looks

classic, clean-cut, and slightly nautical.

- To make any suit more modern, opt for flat-front trousers and a nicely tailored, slim-fitting jacket.

- Black or dark gray trousers will look good with most any color combination.

Beachwear

© photo by Positive Light Photography

- As on the gentlemen above, linen drawstring pants and lightweight shirts are breezy and perfectly beach appropriate for a casual tropical wedding.

- Pair a lightweight cotton suit with leather sandals for a ceremony in the sand, or

skip the shoes altogether and celebrate barefoot!

- Don't go so far with this look that your outfit seems sloppy. Strive to look fresh, clean, and casually polished so you look fantastic standing next to your glowing bride.

and unstructured shapes into your wedding day wardrobe, or take a classic outfit and relax the details so you feel right at home at the beach. Go without a tie, roll up the sleeves of your crisp white shirt, and choose dress pants made with a casual fabric.

If honoring your family heritage is important to you, consider incorporating aspects of your national dress into your wedding day attire. In fashion etiquette, traditional dress from any culture is considered a welcome alternative to formal wear. If it reflects who you are as an individual, it will add

wonderful personality, history, and pride to your celebration, and be perfectly appropriate for your wedding.

Military dress uniforms are near and dear to the hearts of the many people throughout the world who have worked hard to earn the honor of wearing them. Each branch of the U.S. military has its own version of dress uniforms appropriate for formal occasions. They have long and interesting histories with special names, classifications, symbolism, and decorations that represent ranking.

National Dress

© photo by Yours by John Photography

- The most popular version of national dress in the United States is the kilt, worn by those with Scottish or Irish heritage as well as those without.

- Auspicious colors can be added to modern formal wear as a symbol of your heritage. A red cum-

merbund, vest, or pocket square could symbolize good luck.

- Men of African descent might wear a dashiki suit or a grand boubou and men with Latin American heritage might wear a guayabera dress shirt.

Uniforms

© photo by John and Joseph Photography

- Military dress uniforms are also known as "full dress," "mess dress," "mess uniform," or "mess kit."

- According to fashion etiquette, a military dress uniform is appropriate to wear at occasions of any level of

formality, even the most formal white-tie events.

- To learn more about the histories and specific regulations of U.S. military dress uniforms, follow the links listed in the Resources section.

79

FINISHING YOUR LOOK
Make a memorable fashion statement with creative accessories

No matter what kind of menswear you choose for your wedding day, your accessories will add personality and put the finishing touch on your look. Gone are the days of ultrastrict fashion etiquette except in the most formal of settings. Outdated rules like never combining navy with black and never layering patterns have fallen by the wayside in favor of tasteful, individual fashion freedom. Embrace the opportunity to play with these details, and give yourself permission to have a little fun with fashion!

Suits and tuxedos are made up of more than just pants and a jacket. Everything from your shirt and tie to your vest, cummerbund, belt, shoes, and coat will need to be chosen, and each piece offers an opportunity for creative self-expression.

Men's jewelry includes classic staples like cuff links, shirt

Apparel Accessories

© photo by La Vie Photography

- Classic dress shoes will never go out of style. Wear shiny black patent leather dress shoes with a tux or formal suit and simply shaped and nicely polished dress shoes with more casual suits.

- Sleek belts should be worn with suits, but tuxedos should be tailored to fit or held up with suspenders.

- In cold weather a topcoat is the appropriate coat to wear with a tuxedo or formal suit. The most classic version is the velvet collared Chesterfield topcoat.

Jewelry Accessories

© photo by Yours by John Photography

- Cuff links worn with French cuffs are a must for men's formal wear. They can be brightly colored and modern, vintage and full of history, whimsical and humorous (like the dog cuff links above), or customized with your initials, monogram, or other favorite detail.

- Wear a dressy wristwatch or carry a vintage pocket watch in your jacket or pants pocket to keep time on your wedding day.

- Shirt studs with matching cuff links look sleek with a tuxedo.

studs, and watches, all of which can be either formal or funky. Choose high-quality pieces that will stand the test of time to be handed down as heirlooms to future generations, or choose trendier items to add an element of fun.

Adding color and other fun extras to your ensemble is one of the easiest and most powerful ways to change up your style. They can be incorporated into nearly any aspect of your attire, and there is no limit to what combinations will work. Coordinate with your wedding colors and the fashions of your wedding party, but be sure to wear something individual to stand out as the man of the hour. Take your time, enjoy the process, and really make your look your own.

For fashion details this specific, purchase them yourself and give them as gifts.

Colorful Options

© photo by Positive Light Photography

- Ties don't have to be black, white, or gray. If you're wearing a suit, experiment with incorporating your wedding colors into your shirt and tie combination.

- A little color can go a long way. To stay formal, add small splashes of color with your boutonniere or accessories. For a more casual look, the sky's the limit, so have fun with it!

- A pocket square adds a vibrant splash of color or a complementary pattern for texture and depth.

Fun Extras

© photo by La Vie Photography

- Instead of traditional black dress socks, go goofy and wear brightly colored or patterned socks with your groomsmen.

- Boutonnieres can be made of more than just flowers. Interesting ferns, feathers, fabrics, jewelry, and even tiny toys can be used to make a one-of-a-kind accessory.

- For guys who are sporty at heart, classic Converse sneakers are a playful choice paired with a suit.

- How about a hat? Visit a specialty hat store to try on dressy options.

WEDDING DAY EVENTS

Stay cool, calm, and collected from your walk down the aisle to your final good-bye

It's your wedding day, all day, so start off with a delicious breakfast and take it slow. If you're not getting married until later in the afternoon, spend some time with the men in your family and the friends in your life. Give your grooms-men their gifts and make a celebratory toast to your friend-ship. Take time to go the extra mile with your grooming.

After all, you're going to be the center of attention and the subject of thousands of photographs.

Be sure you've checked off all the important items from your to-do list. Double-check that you have the marriage license with you and that your best man has the rings. Tuck a hand-kerchief in your pocket in case your fiancée forgets hers. Head

Relax and Get Ready

- Take a short hike or play a round of golf to relax and enjoy the morning.

- Drink plenty of water and take your vitamins. You need lots of energy to make it through the day with enough left to spare for your wedding night.

- If you haven't told your parents that you love them in a while, now is the perfect time to do so.

- Turn off your cell phone and direct folks to call your best man if they need you.

Ceremony Events

- Make the first moment you see your bride really count; take in how precious she is to you and let her know it.

- When your officiant pronounces that you're hus-band and wife, don't rush out too fast. Soak up the excitement of the moment

and walk down the aisle hand in hand.

- If you're scheduled to have your pictures taken right after your ceremony, set aside some time together to connect before your reception begins.

to your ceremony site early to ensure all is unfolding according to plan. Go over your vows if you wrote them yourself.

When the ceremony begins, remember that even though there is an audience, there's only one VIP in the crowd—your fiancée. Look into her eyes when you're saying your vows, and keep your attention focused on her. When it comes time to kiss your bride, really savor the moment.

Once the most important part of your day is done and you're officially married, you can relax and enjoy your party! There will be plenty of friends and vendors there to keep you on track from your first dance to your getaway, and chances are you've been to enough weddings to know exactly what to do. To help ensure your reception is a joy-filled event for everyone, be generous with your thanks, be flexible with your expectations, and show your wife how much you adore her by staying near her side from beginning to end.

Reception Events

© photo by La Vie Photography

- Thank people from the heart. A wedding toast is a special honor, so be sincere with your comments.

- This will be one of the few times in your life when your friends and family will be together in the same place. Make everyone feel welcome by introducing people to one another.

- Let your wife know at least one hundred times how beautiful she looks.

- Dance with your new mother-in-law at least once.

Perfect Party Tips

© photo by GH Kim Photography

- Be a gentleman and remove her garter with class; remember that her parents and grandparents are watching.

- Thank the professionals who serve you and graciously ask for changes if something isn't going your way.

- Dance with your wife even if you usually don't dance at all, and share the first and last dances with her.

- If you'll be drinking, take it easy. You'll host plenty of parties in your lifetime, but hopefully only one wedding.

EXERCISE & NUTRITION

Celebrate this special time in your life by getting into shape and feeling great

Most people could always do a bit more to be healthy, but with your wedding approaching, there has never been a better time to take great care of yourself and enjoy a big dose of TLC. A healthy diet and regular exercise will give you the energy and clarity of mind to be creative and keep track of details as you plan your wedding, and when your big day arrives, you'll feel fit and fabulous when all eyes are on you.

Treat yourself to a healthy diet, which revolves around loads of water, fresh fruits, vegetables, lean proteins, and whole grains. Approach desserts and alcohol with moderation, and take a multivitamin or vitamin supplements if you feel that your diet is lacking in nutrients. If you want to make a big

Balanced Diet

© photo by Junebug Weddings

- Look for brightly colored fruits and vegetables, which are rich in heart-healthy antioxidants.

- Protein keeps you fuller longer, so start your day with eggs, yogurt, or tofu in your breakfast.

- Dark green vegetables like kale, chard, broccoli, and green beans are packed with vitamins, high in fiber, and low in calories, so you'll stay satisfied longer.

- Get quick energy from powerful carbohydrates in whole grains like brown rice, wild rice, whole wheat, and oatmeal.

Nutrition

© photo by Junebug Weddings

- If you live in a northern area and don't see much sun, you may be vitamin D deficient and need vitamin supplements.

- Calcium is very important for bone strength. Eat dairy products, dark leafy greens, beans, or supplements that include vitamin D.

- Woman of childbearing age benefit from getting folate in their diets. Consider supplements if you're not getting enough.

- Salmon, walnuts, and flax-seeds are fantastic sources of omega-3 fatty acids, which are essential for good health.

shift in the way you're living, talk with your doctor or nutritionist to be sure you're on the right path for you.

Get active, have fun, and make yourself feel good! Make time to take a dance class, take a walk, get to the gym, or play your favorite sport, even if your schedule seems unmanageable. The time spent being active will give you energy for all the things on your to-do list. If you could use some motivation and moral support, find a "bridal boot camp" or fitness class for brides to be. There's nothing like good friends to help you reach your goals.

Exercising on your own isn't the only way to go. You both need to feel your best, so why not make it a team effort? Staying active together is a great way to connect, especially now when you have so much to celebrate. It's also a great way to start healthy traditions that you can continue to enjoy all the way through your marriage.

Keep Yourself Active

© photo by Junebug Weddings

- Yoga will strengthen your body as well as calm your mind during this busy time.

- Use exercise as a stress reliever if your schedule begins to feel overwhelming.

- Think about the areas of your body that your wedding dress is going to accentuate and target your strength training so you'll be excited to show them off.

- Take small stretching and movement breaks throughout your workday to maintain good circulation, posture, and strength and to ward off fatigue.

Stay Active Together

© photo by GH Kim Photography

- Teach each other the activities you love and grow your common interests for a long and fun future together.

- Biking, Rollerblading, and hiking are great activities to do as a pair.

- Just getting outside and throwing a Frisbee or taking a walk will get you moving and let you spend quality time together.

- Encourage each other to get enough sleep. Being well rested supports physical and emotional health in a big way.

SAVVY SKIN CARE
Look radiant on your big day with glowing, beautiful skin

Everyone's skin is different, so no two people are guaranteed to love the same products. Finding the skin-care system that's right for you can be a fun and pampering process. Its success goes hand in hand with your healthy lifestyle choices, so take good care of yourself, inside and out.

The same things that are good for our bodies are also good for our skin. Regular exercise pumps blood to the skin, our

body's biggest organ. Good nutrition and lots of water also keep us looking healthy and hydrated. Getting enough sleep gives our skin time to repair and rejuvenate, and steering clear of cigarettes and too much alcohol is a necessity for a glowing complexion.

Beauty products abound for every purpose under the sun. Cover your bases with a complete basic regimen. Find a great

Cleanse

© photo by Junebug Weddings

- Washing your makeup off every night keeps your pores from clogging.

- Washing too often, or with water that's too hot, can strip natural moisture from your skin and dry you out.

- Gel-based cleansers do a better job at removing

makeup, but cream-based cleansers are more moisturizing for dry skin.

- A deep-cleansing facial can work wonders, but leave at least a few days for your skin to recover before your wedding day.

Exfoliate and Tone

© photo by J. Garner Photography

- A regular exfoliating routine will help you look your best and glow with happiness on your wedding day.

- Gentle scrubs with tiny particles and microdermabrasion are great for removing dead cells from your skin's top layer.

- Alpha and beta hydroxy acids and retinoids go one step further, exfoliating as well as helping with the production of collagen.

- Use toners that act as humectants, which help your moisturizer penetrate your skin. Avoid products that contain alcohol.

cleanser to gently remove makeup and toxins morning and night, an exfoliation system to encourage new cells to shine through, and a moisturizer to soften your skin and create a smooth base for your makeup. After that you can focus on any issues that you want to improve. From acne and psoriasis to redness and irritation, there are products and information out there to help treat any issue.

Moisturize

© photo by Junebug Weddings

- For daytime, choose a moisturizer with SPF 30 to protect your skin from everyday sun damage.

- Apply a vitamin- and nutrient-rich moisturizer before going to bed.

- Two-thirds of the body is made up of water. Drink-ing at least eight glasses of this elixir a day is a must for healthy, hydrated skin.

- If you live in an extremely dry climate, use a humidi-fier in your home to add moisture to the air.

Target Specific Issues

© photo by Junebug Weddings

- Treat acne on your shoul-ders, chest, and back with an acne-fighting body wash or body "facials" so you'll feel fabulously confident in your wedding dress.

- For serious issues and the best advice, visit a der-matologist to formulate a skin-care plan.

- Stress can wreak havoc on your skin. Find nourishing ways to relax and enjoy this exciting time.

- Love is a powerful beauty treatment. As the ones getting married, you're guaranteed to look stun-ning on your wedding day, no matter what!

HEALTH & BEAUTY

MAKEUP BASICS

Accentuate your beauty and style with makeup looks that last all day

Whether you love beauty products or rarely wear any at all, finding great makeup and the best way to wear it on your wedding day can really complement your look.

If makeup is your thing, then have fun doing it yourself; get expert advice at your local makeup counter and through online video instruction and forums. If your interests lie elsewhere, a professional makeup artist can be an invaluable investment. With his or her technical know-how and artistic abilities, he or she can create a look that's both beautiful and practical and makes you feel like the very best version of you.

You will be photographed all day, so you need to choose

Glowing Skin

© photo by Junebug Weddings

- Your makeup will look best if your skin is happy. Finish beauty treatments twenty-four to forty-eight hours prior to your wedding day to allow time to ease any redness.

- If you have sensitive skin, look for products made with natural ingredients and that are hypoallergenic or noncomedogenic.

- Be sure to moisturize well before applying your makeup.

- Start with a concealer or light base to even out your skin tone and cover up blemishes.

Classic Makeup

© photo by Junebug Weddings

- Lightly line your eyes in black or brown or use a liquid liner to create a more defined line and give a slightly vintage effect.

- Brown eye shadow in the crease of your eyelid and a lighter shadow highlighting your brow bone will accentuate your eye's natural shape.

- Simple pink cheeks and a classic red lip will never go out of style. Try out different shades of red lipstick to find the shade that complements your skin tone.

products that will look great on film and hold up to long hours of wear. Outdoor weddings are photographed in natural light, so you'll look best with more natural-style makeup, tones that complement your coloring and nothing too extreme. Indoor weddings often require flash photography and artificial lighting, so avoid products with SPF, as they may reflect light in an artificial-looking way. Camera flashes can also bring out redness in lighter skin, so be sure to create a good base and cover up any redness in your skin with the proper tones of concealer or foundation.

HEALTH & BEAUTY

Casual Makeup

© photo by Junebug Weddings

- Show off your natural beauty with makeup that looks barely there.

- Gently shimmering products can give your skin a little extra life, but overdoing it may make you appear shiny in your photos.

- Pinks and earth tones are nice warm neutrals that will give you a rosy, healthy glow. Play to find the shades that work for you.

- Choose a creamy lipstick that enhances your natural lip color, or go for a simple translucent lip gloss.

Dramatic Makeup

© photo by Junebug Weddings

- Smoky eyes with gray, brown, or even rich plum or navy liner and shadow are dramatic statements for fashion-forward brides.

- False eyelashes add instant glamour and definition in photographs. Use a short strip of graduated-length lashes on the outer half of each eye, or add a few individual lashes for the most natural look.

- Choose one area of the face to focus on so you never look overdone. Go for a dramatic eye with a neutral lip, or vice versa.

89

HAIRSTYLES

Find the perfect hairstyle to match your look, from dramatically chic to naturally beautiful

Your hair is one of your most important accessories for your wedding day, and there can be a great number of ways to wear it, depending on its length and thickness. Look to the general style of your wedding for inspiration, as well as specific fashion items like your wedding dress, jewelry, veil, or hair accessories.

Practicality can also play a part in your hairstyle decision. If you're getting married in a hot climate, you may not want to wear your hair down on your neck; if you'll be somewhere breezy, choose a natural style that will look nice a bit tousled.

In the midst of your wedding planning, remember to take care of your hair and make appointments for all the

Classic Hairstyles

© photo by Junebug Weddings

- A low chignon at the nape of your neck, as shown above, is universally flattering and an eternally classic look.

- If your hair isn't very long, but you'd like an updo, try temporary natural hair extensions or hairpieces.

- A simple updo at the crown of your head looks lovely with a veil placed either above or below it.

- A French twist is another classic hairstyle that looks beautiful from every angle and can accommodate many different types of veils and hair accessories.

Casual Hairstyles

© photo by Junebug Weddings

- Wear your hair down in smooth waves like the bride in the photo for a naturally romantic look, or go sleek and straighten your hair to add a modern edge.

- Wear your hair half up and half down for an option that's pretty but not too formal.

- To look most like yourself, try a twist on your everyday style. Choose your favorite look and add a little extra polish.

- Add the finishing touch to your casual do with an anti-frizz serum or shine spray.

maintenance you'll need leading up to your big day. If you color your hair, have it freshened up a week or two ahead of time, and unless you're really daring, don't go for any major changes right before your wedding.

Have fun experimenting with different looks, and ask a friend to take photos of you from different angles if you're trying to decide between options. Take photos of your look once you've decided on it so you'll have an easy reference point for other fashion purchases.

Vintage or Retro Hairstyles

© photo by Junebug Weddings

- A 1940s-inspired updo with rolling waves and dramatic shape like the one shown above creates a fun backdrop for sparkling hair accessories.

- Finger waves with a bob or shorter haircut is a look inspired by the 1920s.

- Find your favorite vintage look and work with your hairstylist to create a flattering updated version.

- For subtlety, balance a modern wedding dress with a vintage hairstyle, or a vintage dress with a modern do.

Alternative Hairstyles

© photo by Junebug Weddings

- A little height in a hairstyle can make a simple look more dramatic.

- Ponytails are playful and can be worn high, low, or off to the side.

- Let your chosen hair accessory or veil inspire a hairstyle that you will absolutely love.

- Be careful not to choose something too trendy that will quickly look dated. No one wants to look back on their wedding photos years down the road and wonder what they were thinking.

FINISHING YOUR LOOK
Pamper yourself, polish your look, and stay beautiful all day long

Putting the finishing touch on your wedding day style is all about paying attention to the details. From the tip of your toes to the top of your head, think of ways to pamper yourself and polish your look.

Keep in mind that beauty extras that are seemingly small can make a big difference. The same way that a few extra eyelashes can add big impact, so can whiter teeth, a healthy

bronzed glow from a spray tan, and a glossing treatment to your hair. Romantic touches like special scents and perfumes and small nostalgic accessories can add much to the day's meaning and help to make memories. Think about the little things you love to have around you and choose a few to wear or carry with you.

The days leading up to your wedding are sure to be full of

Beauty Extras

- Temporary false lashes like the ones above create instant glamour and are easy to apply and remove.

- Professionally applied eyelash extensions give you weeks of thick, full lashes. Consider getting them for a low-maintenance look on your wedding day as well as

on your honeymoon.

- Treat yourself to some new makeup and beauty products.

- A body lotion with a slight shimmer can be a lovely touch on bare arms, shoulders, and collarbones.

Makeup Touch-ups

- Blotting papers work wonders for shiny foreheads, noses, and chins, for both the bride and groom. Keep them handy so you'll always look picture-perfect.

- Lipstick will fade throughout the day, especially if there is a good amount of

kissing going on! Keep lip pencil, lipstick, or lip gloss with you for touch-ups.

- Ask one of your brides- maids to be in charge of carrying your makeup and letting you know when you could use a little freshening up.

activity, so be sure to treat yourself gently and get in some quality rest and relaxation whenever you can. A day or two before your wedding, visit a spa and get a massage, facial, manicure, and pedicure to give your body a beautiful boost and help melt away your stress. Remember to laugh freely, breathe deeply, and let your beauty shine through.

These days spa treatments aren't just for girls; both of you can benefit. If the groom isn't much of a "spa guy," surprise him with a gift of a massage at his sports club or at a massage therapy center. If you don't think he'll enjoy going it alone,

make it an event you share and book a couple's massage or other decadent couple's treatment. If you're headed for a tropical honeymoon, find a package that incorporates techniques or ingredients from the region you're heading to for a nice sneak peek at what's to come.

Perfume

© photo by Yours by John Photography

- Chose a special new perfume to represent your wedding day and have sweet memories of your celebration every time you put it on.

- The sense of smell is a powerful one and has strong ties to emotions and memories.

- If there is a scent you wear every day, don't forget to bring it along if you're getting ready away from home.

- If you're not a perfume wearer, choose flowers for your bouquet that have a natural scent you love.

Manicures and Pedicures

© photo by J. Garner Photography

- If you're not big on nail color, try a simple French manicure or coat of clear polish.

- Getting a manicure and pedicure is the perfect way to be pampered the day before your wedding. You get time to sit and relax, and your nails will be ready for their close-up.

- Make manicures and pedicures a group event. Take along the ladies in your wedding party for some prewedding fun. Or invite your mother and new mother-in-law for quality family bonding time.

WEDDING DAY SURVIVAL KIT

Come prepared for life's little "emergencies" with your own bridal tool kit

With all the hustle and bustle a wedding day brings, there are sure to be moments when you need some helpful supplies to assist with the issue at hand. Thinking ahead and either purchasing or putting together a good collection of beauty, health, and emergency items to have available on your wedding day will save you lots of worry and may, in fact, save the day!

A lot of thought has gone into getting your look just right for your wedding, but if your day begins early and your celebration ends late, you will probably need to freshen up your hair and makeup at some point to stay looking your best. Just a few beauty basics can really come in handy.

If you're getting dressed and ready at a hotel or another

Freshening Up

© photo by Junebug Weddings

- Basic makeup supplies like concealer, powder, blush, and lip gloss always come in handy for touch-ups.

- Pack small bottles of hairspray, bobby pins, barrettes, and hair bands in case someone's hairdo needs a little assistance.

- If your wedding is in the hot summer months, have simple folding paper fans available to help keep everyone cool.

- Bring along your toothbrush, or at least some breath mints, so you're confident when it's time to kiss the bride.

In Case of Emergency

© photo by Junebug Weddings

- "Emergency" extras like pain relievers, antacids, feminine hygiene products, and deodorant are all worth having nearby, just in case.

- A collection of various supplies like tissues, cotton swabs, eyedrops, nail files, and drinking straws are smart additions that are nice to have when you need them.

- Just a touch of clear nail polish can stop pantyhose from running and the ends of ribbon from unraveling.

- Pack Band-Aids, sports tape, or moleskin to help ward off blisters.

location away from home, you may miss some of the every-day items you keep in your medicine cabinet but rarely think about as important. To ward off headaches, settle the butter-flies in your stomach, file a broken nail, moisten dry contacts, or take care of any other common occurrences, keep a collection of "emergency" supplies available for the both of you, your family, and your wedding party.

As you're planning the schedule for your wedding day, don't forget to consider what you're going to eat before your reception. Your wedding day is no time to run on an empty stomach! Make yummy snacks for everyone part of the fun of getting ready and you'll have a wedding party that's happy, with energy to spare.

Straps break, buttons fall off, and invariably a groomsman forgets his socks. Be sure you have a basic sewing kit on hand as well as other supplies like pins, tape, stain remover, and, of course, black men's dress socks, for easy fashion fixes.

Take Care of Yourself

© photo by La Vie Photography

- Have plenty of water on hand for the two of you, your family, and your wedding party so no one gets dehydrated.

- Plan to have food available, but put someone else in charge of transporting it.

- Even if nerves have made you lose your appetite, eat anyway to help maintain your energy.

- Be extra careful not to go overboard with your alcohol consumption if you're enjoying celebratory drinks.

Your Sewing Kit

© photo by Junebug Weddings

- A simple sewing kit containing needles, scissors, and both light and dark thread can be a lifesaver for loose buttons, broken straps, and falling hems.

- Safety pins in numerous sizes are multipurpose tools for fashion or decor hiccups.

- White chalk can be used to temporarily color over many stains on a white wedding dress.

- Double-sided tape is helpful for keeping plunging necklines and loose straps under control.

DRESS SHAPES

Create a stunning silhouette with a dress shape that flatters your figure

When it comes to weddings, there's nothing more iconic than the image of the bride in her wedding dress. Flooded with history, symbolism, and emotion, your dress is one of the biggest style statements and most fun fashion choices you'll make in your lifetime. To make the process of finding your dress a stress-free experience, consider the following:

your wedding theme, your color palette, the time of year, and your personal style. Begin with the basics of dress shape so you're sure to find one that fits and flatters.

Ball gowns are inspired by the most formal and romantic of events and lend an air of fairy-tale splendor. A-line dresses are classic with versatile shapes, their skirts form a simple

Ball Gown

© photo by Junebug Weddings

- Ball gowns are made with many layers of fabric and petticoats and can have an overlay of tulle or other sheer embroidered fabric.

- Some ball gown skirts have varying numbers of "pick-ups" or gathers in order to make the skirt look fuller and more textured.

- With the full shape of most ball gown skirts beginning at the natural waist or just below, these dresses look best on brides who want to draw attention to their upper bodies.

A-Line

© photo by Junebug Weddings

- A-line skirts create a slimming silhouette that flatters most every body type.

- An A-line dress with an empire waist beginning just below the bust will bring the focus up toward the chest, shoulders, and face and hide an undefined or fuller waist.

- If the A-line skirt begins at the true waist, it will show off a classic and sweetly symmetrical silhouette.

- Drop-waisted dresses accentuate a long lean body or an evenly proportioned hourglass figure.

triangular line, and their waistlines can begin high, middle, or low depending on your frame. Mermaid-shaped dresses are the exaggerated version of a drop-waisted dress, and their body-hugging lines add drama to your look. Sheath dresses are the simplest in their construction, but they can have big fashion impact and fantastic fit.

Try on something from each category to see what flatters your form. Then choose the one dress that has the fit, fabric, and flair to make you truly feel like a bride.

Mermaid

© photo by Junebug Weddings

- Mermaid dresses will bring out the curves in a slim figure.

- Extra texture can be created and flaws hidden with gathers and ruches in the fabric of the bodice.

- When trying on your mermaid dress, walk around a bit to be sure the skirt isn't too tight to move in comfortably.

- Avoid the mermaid dress if your body is pear-shaped or heavier on the bottom than on the top.

Sheath

© photo by Junebug Weddings

- Sheath dresses closely follow the lines of the body and are best made with fabrics that drape well.

- Bias-cut dresses are slim and sexy and create a glamorous look perfect for a more vintage style.

- Choose a sheath dress in a simple fabric for a casual, clean style, or try an embellished fabric with spectacular details for a formal, sophisticated look.

- The uncluttered lines of a sheath dress make a beautiful base for captivating accessories.

YOUR DRESS

NECKLINES
Choose a picture-perfect neckline for a day when all eyes are on you

Once you have an idea of the type of dress shape that works best on you, the next thing to consider is the neckline. The neckline is the frame for your face that guides the eye toward your features while giving your dress unique personality.

Strapless dresses are the new classics and they're designed in every dress shape and style available. Look for a version that flatters your particular build, whether curvy or petite, and be sure it is constructed to stay in place comfortably. V-neck and halter-neck dresses can also be combined with several different dress shapes, and the shoulder straps and neck fasteners that are used to hold them up provide extra support for figures that need it. The right shaped V-neck can either lessen the look of a full-size bust or show off the curves you want revealed. Off-the-shoulder, portrait, illusion, and bateau

Strapless and Spaghetti Strap

© photo by Junebug Weddings

- Slim, angular figures can wear straight strapless necklines, but slight curves, scallops, or sweetheart necklines are the most flattering options.

- Spaghetti straps look best on petite frames, and wider straps look best on voluptuous figures.

- The spacing of straps can change a neckline dramatically. Look at several versions to see what you like best.

- Detailed gathers and folds at the top of a strapless dress are called "crumb-catchers" and add architectural interest to a neckline.

V-Neck and Halter

© photo by Junebug Weddings

- V-necks create a long vertical line that draws the eye up and down, creating a slimmer appearance.

- Deep V-necks can be dramatic and sexy, but only if you feel comfortable and confident and your dress fits you to a T.

- Halter-neck dresses emphasize lovely arms and shoulders and can show a little or a lot of your back.

- Experiment with the many styles of halter necks to find one that flatters your face and features the most.

or Sabrina necklines are feminine, romantic, and graceful, flattering and framing shoulders and pretty collarbones.

Whether you go with a classic shape, square neck, scoop neck, Victorian collar, or asymmetrical design, find the one that makes the most of your features while complementing the shape of your skirt. There's a beautiful dress out there waiting for you to find it!

ZOOM

After the wedding your dress should be professionally dry-cleaned by a specialist and stored in a sturdy acid-free cardboard box or hung on a padded hanger inside a breathable fabric garment bag. Plastic bags won't let air circulate and can trap moisture in the fabric, causing mold, discoloration, and deterioration.

Off-the-Shoulder Options

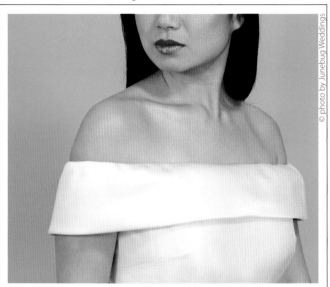

© photo by Junebug Weddings

- Off-the-shoulder necklines, like the one shown above, accentuate beautiful shoulders, collarbones, and arms.

- Bateau necklines stop right at the outside edge of the shoulder blade and don't fall lower onto the arm.

- Portrait collars are made of wide swaths of fabric and perfectly frame the face and upper body.

- All of these neckline options look lovely with cap sleeves, three-quarter-length sleeves, long sleeves, or no sleeves at all.

Alternatives

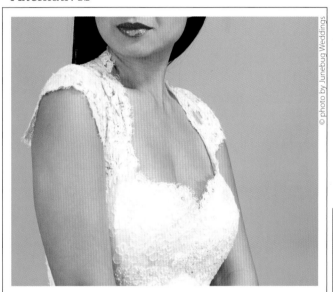

© photo by Junebug Weddings

- Illusion necklines give the suggestion of sheer fabric but cover you up in all the right places. The one shown above is double layered over the bust but sheer lace over the back and shoulders.

- Asymmetrical necklines look ultramodern while harkening back to traditional Grecian style.

- Scoop necks can be made as higher rounded jewel necks or plunging dramatic curves, with similar or more dramatic shapes echoed in the back of your dress.

YOUR DRESS

CLASSIC DRESSES

Classic tailoring, traditional accents, and formal fabrics combine to create a timeless look

"Here comes the bride, all dressed in white!" Classic dress styles are timeless and elegant and look beautiful on brides the world over. If your vision is transforming into a modern-day princess at an elegant white wedding, then a classic wedding dress is for you.

Classic wedding gowns can come in a variety of shapes,

though the colors are generally limited to shades of white and cream. Beautiful embellishments like beading, embroidery, sequins, and crystals add formality to these structured, dramatic dresses, and the fabrics used are lush and luxurious.

Wedding dress boutiques and bridal salons specialize in matching brides to their dresses, so their expert staffs can be

Colors

© photo by J. Garner Photography

- A satin sash in a refined light color such as taupe or pale pink can add a formal touch of color without looking too trendy.

- Classic dresses are either true white, natural white, or cream, with subtle colored accents, if any.

- Look to your shoes and accessories to add hints of color to a classic white dress.

- Introduce color with a brooch of colored stones at your waist, bust, or shoulder straps.

Embellishments

© photo by La Vie Photography

- Tone-on-tone beading and embroidery add sparkling embellishments without changing your dress color.

- Silver, gold, or bronze embellishments are perfect for winter weddings.

- Be careful when having your dress cleaned. Beading

and embellishments can be damaged by the chemicals, so talk with your cleaning professional about safety precautions.

- Bring along a sewing kit on your wedding day in case embellishments loosen and need repair.

invaluable resources in helping you find the one dress that is right for you. Familiarize yourself with the basics in fit and style, then make an appointment at a few of your area's bridal boutiques and let the professionals work their magic. Experienced salespeople will be well educated in their field and will ask you important questions about what you're envisioning for your big day in order to guide you toward the best dresses to try on. Take their expert advice, but remember to take things slowly. Ultimately you are the expert on what makes you feel fabulous.

Fabrics

© photo by La Vie Photography

- Popular laces used in wedding dresses are alençon, battenburg, Chantilly, French, guipure, point d'esprit, and Schiffli.

- High-quality wedding dress fabrics are mostly made of silk but can also include silk and polyester blends as well as fine cotton.

- Rich fabrics like satin and taffeta are perfect for the formal beauty of classic dresses.

- Full skirts in a ball gown or A-line dress may have layers of net, tulle, organza, or chiffon.

Considerations

© photo by La Vie Photography

YOUR DRESS

- Bring one or two trusted friends or family members along while you shop so you feel supported but not overwhelmed.

- Don't buy the first dress you try on or feel pressured to buy one the very first day. Returns can be difficult, so sleep on it and be sure of your decision.

- Most formal wedding dresses are custom made to your measurements, so order yours six to twelve months in advance to allow for construction and multiple fittings and alterations.

CASUAL DRESSES

Creative fabrics and playful details create dress styles that feel as good as they look

Casual wedding dresses are for brides who want to give classic wedding traditions their own personal twist. Wear a lovely tea-length dress for your afternoon garden wedding, a ball gown with dramatic black-and-white details for your masquerade-themed gala, or an ultramodern body-hugging sheath for your urban-chic event. Just use your imagination

and discover what represents you most authentically.

There are no color restrictions for a casual gown, and more and more designers are experimenting with shades from pale blue to hot pink and everything in between. Color can be incorporated into the construction of your dress or added on after the fact to add flourish and a fun-loving flair to your

Colors

© photo by Positive Light Photography

- Be bold with splashes of color. The bride above chose a simple white dress to show off purple accents in her hair, bouquet, makeup, and decor.

- Coordinate your dress colors and accessories with your groom's look and the rest of your wedding party fashion.

- Choose a champagne, pink, or taupe dress instead of the traditional white.

- Give a white wedding dress a fresh look by adding colorful jewelry and accessories for your reception.

Embellishments

© photo by La Vie Photography

- As in the photo above, ruffles or lace trim at the hem of your dress can finish off your look with flourish.

- Gathered fabric flowers decorating your neck, shoulders, waistline, or bustle are simple but dramatic feminine touches.

- Layering sheer and patterned fabrics together is another fun way to create depth, texture, and a sculptural quality to your dress.

- Ribbon detailing along your neckline and shoulders will add delicate interest and creates a flattering frame for your face.

look. Embellishments come in all shapes and sizes and aren't limited to traditional materials. The textures of feathers, felt, and unfinished edges combine with formal wedding fabrics like satin, lace, and chiffon to gorgeous effect, and nontraditional fabrics can make wonderfully unique wedding dresses all on their own. Incorporate personal fashion accents, let yourself be inspired by the things you love as well as the style and theme of your wedding day, and you'll have a wedding dress that is anything but ordinary.

Fabrics

© photo by La Vie Photography

- Combine fabrics like the lace and taffeta combination shown above.

- Wedding dresses don't have to be made of silk; fine cotton dresses in dotted point d'esprit or a sweet summery eyelet are wonderful choices for warm weather weddings.

- Comfort is the key to an enjoyable day. Move around in your dress to be sure you feel as great as you look.

- Whimsical embroidery in leaf, floral, and vine motifs can add interest to your fabric choices.

Considerations

© photo by Barbie Hull Photography

- Consider your wedding location and season when choosing your dress. An ultraformal and heavy dress will feel uncomfortable out in the sunshine on a warm day like the one shown above.

- Play up the theme of your wedding with the style and details of your dress.

- Trunk shows at bridal boutiques allow you to see the entire dress collection at once and sometimes even meet the designers themselves.

- Many dress shops have sample sales where you can buy standard-size floor samples at a discount.

YOUR DRESS

VINTAGE DRESSES

Evoke an era of romance with an heirloom or vintage wedding gown

The romance, nostalgia, and dramatic flair of a vintage wedding dress show off a unique style that can't be compared. From Victorian dresses with regal high collars to the playful retro dresses of the 1950s and 1960s, there are vintage styles to suit every taste.

To find the dress that suits you best, do a little research into dress shops in your area as well as online. Contact the managers of your favorite stores and let them know what you're looking for so they can contact you when a great find comes in. Vintage sizes can be small, and it may take some time to find the dress you're dreaming of, but with a little persistence and creative thinking there are lots of options available.

If you're lucky the dress of your dreams may already be in

1940s and Before

© photo by Cheri Pearl Photography

- Slinky bias-cut dresses in silk charmeuse that showed off the body's form, similar to the one shown above, ruled the 1930s and 1940s.

- Dresses in the 1920s had looser-fitting drop waists and beautiful beading and embroidery.

- Dress sizes have changed over time, so pay attention to a garment's measurements, not the size on its tag.

- It's difficult to find a dress from before 1930 that's in good enough shape to wear. Consider a reproduction instead.

1950s, 1960s, and 1970s Retro

© photo by La Vie Photography

- Elegant and mod, the style of the late 1960s and 70s included long column dresses and empire waists like the slightly Grecian inspired dress above.

- Cinched waists and full skirts typify a classic look of the 1950s and early 1960s.

- Buy vintage dresses from trusted, expert shop owners and ask lots of questions about the garment's condition, sizing, and repair history before you buy.

- Be sure you're crystal clear on the return policy if buying a vintage dress online.

your family. If you'd love to wear your mother's or grand-mother's wedding dress, there are many ways to alter its fit or update its look so that it looks like it was made for you. If big alterations are what you want, be sure the dress' owner understands your plans and agrees to them.

Another way to wear the most stylish of vintage wedding dresses is to buy a reproduction dress inspired by the era you love most, or to make a new dress out of a vintage pattern.

Heirloom Wedding Dress

© photo by Positive Light Photography

- This bride had her mother's dress altered to wear on her own modern wedding day.

- If someone you love allows you to alter her dress to be your own, treat it and her offer with the utmost care.

- Extend the waist of a short-waisted vintage dress by adding a wide fabric sash to the dress's middle or reat-taching the skirt higher up.

- Seam allowances in the torso can often be let out for a better fit around the rib cage.

Vintage-Inspired Reproductions

© photo by Junebug Weddings

- A vintage-inspired dress gives you a dramatic look without the challenges involved with real vintage clothing.

- If you're having a custom dress designed, ask your dressmaker to build a mus-lin mock-up of your dress before he or she cuts into the final fabric. This way you can fix any major issues with the fit first.

- You're not limited to only vintage wedding dress pat-terns. Choose any vintage dress pattern you like and use luxurious white fabrics to make it look bridal.

YOUR DRESS

ALTERNATIVE DRESSES

Make a fresh fashion statement with a dress that's out of the ordinary

A traditional white wedding dress may not appeal to you if you're a bride with a distinct sense of your own personal style, so don't feel pressured to conform. Choose a dress that matches your personality, creates a fashion statement, and makes you feel as beautiful and blissful on the outside as you do in your heart.

Choose colors you have a strong personal connection with or ones that are symbolic of qualities you admire. Cool colors like blues and greens are calming and can represent nature. Warm colors like reds, pinks, and oranges are energizing and can represent romance, joy, and prosperity. If you choose a dress that's less bridal than most, use fashionable

Colors

© photo by Stephanie Cristalli Photography

- Who says you have to wear only white to your wedding? Add bold splashes of color like the bride shown above.

- Choose a little black dress, a rich red ball gown, a patterned mini, or any color dress you love to wear.

- For a beach wedding wear a sea blue dress that accentuates your surroundings.

- For a garden wedding wear a floral sundress in tones that match the season's blossoms while highlighting your natural beauty.

Embellishments

© photo by GH Kim Photography

- Give a nod to your heritage with ethnically important details, patterns, and embellishments.

- Both live flowers and fabric flowers can be fashioned onto a sash or clipped to your dress's neckline, shoulder straps, or waistband.

- Embroidery can be bright and bold or subtle and sophisticated. Use it to add interest and beauty to your dress.

- Creative construction including pleats, folds, unfinished edges, and elaborate seams add complexity to a simple design.

embellishments and accessories to add in wedding style. A fabric flower trim or sparkling embroidery across your neckline will add a formal touch and make you stand out in the crowd. Fabrics communicate style and personality with their flow, texture, and feel, so play up your fabric's qualities to purposely soften or strengthen your look. Try on dresses with different shapes and structures to find the style that suits you best. Think outside the box and shop at all kinds of stores to find what you're looking for. You never know where inspiration may strike!

ZOOM

During your dress alteration sessions, bring along your wedding shoes and appropriate undergarments to get the correct hem length and fit. Count on having at least two sessions with your seamstress or tailor for basic adjustments, or more for extensive restructuring or rebuilding.

Fabrics

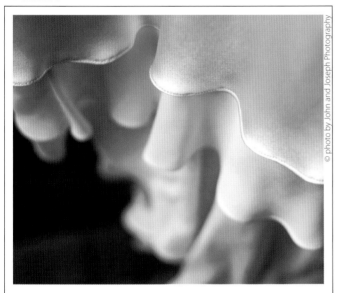

© photo by John and Joseph Photography

- The silk charmeuse in the photo above has a lovely sheen and will drape smoothly and dramatically against your skin for a glamorous look.

- Silk chiffon is soft and airy and looks beautiful gathered and layered—perfect for a Grecian-style dress.

- Velvet, devore (or burnout) velvet, damask, and brocade make luxurious fabric choices for winter weddings.

- Linen and cotton fabrics like eyelet, matelassé, organdy, seersucker, and twill are fresh and feminine for summertime weddings.

Considerations

© photo by Jenny Jimenez Photography

- Keep an open mind and trust your instincts. No one knows your personal style better than you do!

- If you buy your dress off the rack, find a good tailor to work with so the fit feels custom made.

- Wear a bridesmaid's dress in white or another color you love, for a casual yet wedding-appropriate look.

- Let yourself daydream about your wedding day and take note of the pictures that materialize— that's probably a look worth searching for.

YOUR DRESS

LINGERIE & UNDERPINNINGS

Smooth body shapers and lovely, lacy undergarments keep you feeling poised and pretty

Your dress is destined to be the most talked-about piece of your wedding wardrobe, but it's what's underneath that will make it fit and make you look fabulous. Throughout history women have loved lingerie for its beauty as well as its lifting, flattening, and corseting effects that helped them create the desired silhouette of the times. Now it's your turn to define your shape by adding some sweet and sexy things to your wedding wardrobe.

For your big day you may want lingerie that helps smooth and shape you for a flattering look. There are all sorts of strapless bras and body shapers made specifically to wear underneath bridal looks, available at department stores.

Structural Underpinnings

© photo by Junebug Weddings

- Strapless bras and bustiers like this one can add structure and shape beneath form-fitting gowns and help keep them securely in place.

- Backless and halter dresses need bras with convertible straps or silicone bra cups that adhere directly to the skin.

- Body shapers are available to smooth any problem areas you might have: tummy, thighs, bottom, back, and more.

- Take your undergarments with you for dress fittings and alteration sessions.

Sexy Extras

© photo by Positive Light Photography

- You don't have to wear just white. If your dress has many layers, sexy, colorful lingerie adds playful personality to your look, and can be your "something blue."

- Anything goes underneath your wedding dress, so have fun with the fashion of it; no one will see it but you and your new husband.

- Personalized panties with your husband's name, your married name, or your monogram embroidered or spelled out in crystals are a fun surprise for later in the night.

To have fun with what you're wearing underneath, try a traditional garter, pretty stockings, or colorful, lacy personalized panties. The garter is meant for the groom to throw to his single male guests, so you may decide to wear two: one for holding on to as a keepsake and one to be thrown to determine which man will marry next. When your reception is over, your wedding night will provide the ideal opportunity to have fun with lingerie, so treat yourself to something special that makes you feel sexy and beautiful.

Garters

© photo by Junebug Weddings

- The garter can easily be your "something old" if you have the one your mother or grandmother wore to her own wedding.

- Long ago it was considered good luck for wedding guests to have a piece of the bride's clothing, so the tossing of the bouquet and garter began.

- You can wear a garter purely for fashion fun, even if you don't want your groom to throw it during the reception.

Wedding Night Lingerie

© photo by Junebug Weddings

- Whether it's your first night together or your four hundredth, your wedding night happens once in a lifetime, so make it special with lingerie just for the occasion.

- A lovely slip or negligee will come in handy for lounging in your hotel room or on your honeymoon.

- Surprise him with super-sexy pieces that you know he'll love to see you in.

- Choose lingerie that makes you feel confident, sensual, and stunning, no matter what your personal style.

FASHION

VEILS

From full-length to fingertip, veils offer a finishing touch that transforms you into a bride

Wedding veils have been used throughout time to symbolize cultural and spiritual beliefs and wishes. While today some brides wear a veil as a symbol, most brides wear one to make a fabulous fashion statement. Veils come in all shapes, lengths, and styles and act like a little bit of fashion magic as they instantly transform a woman into a bride.

Depending on the shape and style of your wedding dress and the level of formality of your celebration, you'll want to choose a veil that accentuates your dress's features and adds a finishing touch to your look. Mantilla veils can be made of lace, tulle, or chiffon and generally have beautifully embellished edges. They were originally made popular in Spain in the 1800s, and

Mantilla

© photo by Junebug Weddings

- Mantilla veils are fastened to your hair with a simple comb or hairpins.

- They are traditionally positioned to lay gently on top of your head with the lace or scalloped edges delicately framing your face and shoulders.

- Because mantilla veils are embellished with detailed lace, embroidery, and decorative edging, they often look best with simple wedding gowns.

- Cut in a round or oval shape, they can be any length from shoulder to cathedral.

Fingertip and Elbow Length

© photo by La Vie Photography

- Short, full bouffant-style veils add a fun and whimsical look to your day.

- Elbow-length and fingertip veils are amazingly versatile and are exactly as long as their names imply.

- The blusher is the layer of the veil worn forward over

the face. Traditionally your father will lift your veil as he gives you away, or your groom will lift it just before the kiss.

- Ribbon, jewels, or other embellishments often line the edges of classic veils.

they still lend a romantic quality to bridal looks.

Classic wedding veils can be gathered and fastened at the top of the head, at the back of the head, or at the nape of the neck, depending on your hairstyle and neckline. They come in a wide variety of fabrics, shapes, and lengths and beautifully complement any bride's style. Cage- or birdcage-style veils are retro inspired and made of sheer netting or tulle. They are dramatic, stylish, and perfect for a fashion-forward bride.

Full Length

© photo by J. Garner Photography

- Full-length or cathedral-length veils add traditional formality and grandeur to your wedding look.

- Full-length veils can have delicate embellishments or embroidery that accentuates their dramatic length and beauty.

- Most full-length veils create a train that will flow behind you and look wonderful as you walk down the aisle.

- Consider wearing a full-length veil during the wedding ceremony but trading it for a decorative hair accessory at the reception for ease of movement.

Cage Style

© photo by Junebug Weddings

- Lengths vary, but cage veils generally hit just below your eyes or just beneath your chin.

- Fabric flowers, feathers, or other decorative hair jewels look great attached to a cage veil where the fabric gathers and attaches to the hair.

- Small rhinestones or pearls can be added to the veil's edges or to the crossing point of the netting for extra sparkle and glamour.

- Cage veils look best with vintage-inspired or fashion-forward wedding dresses.

FASHION

HAIR ACCESSORIES

Jewels, fabrics, feathers, and flowers offer fabulous hairstyle accents

Hair accessories offer an infinite variety of fun and fashionable options to add to your wedding day look. From jewels and vintage hair combs to fresh flowers and DIY creations, there are unending options! Use one to add a bit more embellishment to your hairstyle, to wear on its own if a traditional white wedding veil just isn't you, or for replacing your veil during your reception as a more casual and party-appropriate accessory.

Wearing a real flower in your hair is a romantic look that will never go out of style. Whether you choose one large flower or a grouping of many small ones, their natural beauty will always enhance yours. Choose flowers that echo those in your bouquet or coordinate with your wedding colors. Each flower has a traditional meaning, so you may want to choose ones that represent qualities you hold dear.

Real Flowers

© photo by Junebug Weddings

- Tuck a single large flower like a lily, orchid, or hibiscus behind one ear for an exotic look, perfect for a summer or beach wedding.

- Daisies and baby roses are often long lasting outside of water and won't easily wilt.

- Red, yellow, pink, or white roses tucked in or around an updo are classic and romantic and easy to find year-round.

- Purchase extra blooms and keep them refrigerated so you can replace wilting hair flowers during your reception if necessary.

Tiaras and Jewels

© photo by Junebug Weddings

- Tiaras and jeweled hair accessories are very versatile. They look beautiful worn with a veil and look lovely on their own during your reception once you remove your veil.

- Consider using a vintage brooch or other piece of

sparkling jewelry as a hair accessory; fasten it securely to your hair with hairpins.

- Get creative; most jeweled hair clips can be worn in many different positions depending on your hairstyle. Experiment to find the look you like best.

Traditional tiaras or creative jeweled hairpins are glamorous additions to any hairstyle and can easily be worn with or without a veil. Tiaras sit atop your head and lend a look of royalty, while accessories in all sorts of other shapes and sizes, new or vintage, can be worn to add sparkle and brilliance around your face.

Headbands can be worn with long flowing locks, simple updos, or shorter hairstyles and are universally flattering no matter what your hair length or face shape. They can be made of anything—fabric, lace, jewels, or metals—and they portray a sweet and youthful femininity.

Creative designs featuring fabric flowers, feathers, beads, crystals, and other beautiful materials are widely available today at dress shops, online stores, and fashionable boutiques. Making one you love could also be a fun DIY project if you want to get more involved in putting a personal touch on your wedding day fashion.

Headbands

© photo by Junebug Weddings

- If you're having your dress custom made or significantly altered, find out if there is extra fabric left over that could be made into a simple, elegant headband.

- Add color to your look with a headband that matches your wedding and flower colors.

- A jeweled necklace could be used as a headband by pinning it to your hair or adding a section of elastic to its ends.

- Consider headbands for your bridesmaids for a nicely coordinated look.

Fabric and Feather Creations

© photo by Junebug Weddings

- Fabric flowers can be made more formal by adding sparkling crystals to their edges or centers.

- For a more dramatic look, long feathers can create height and movement in a creative hair accessory.

- Explore fabric stores and look at their selections of ribbons, lace, fabrics, feathers, and notions to find creative DIY inspiration.

- Anything goes! Let your imagination run wild and create something that is as unique and beautiful as you are.

SHOES

Put your best foot forward with shoes that accent your dress and your style

Your wedding dress will most likely be the starting point for your wedding day fashion, but it's easy and fun to add on to your look from there by playing with your accessory choices. Shoes are perfect to liven up your style without straying too far from your comfort zone. They're hidden under your dress but make delicate and dramatic special appearances as you walk down the aisle, twirl on the dance floor, and give a little jump for joy. For the most successful result consider the look you're going for as well as your practical needs.

If you live in an area where there aren't many shopping options for formal shoes, explore the many online boutiques. Shopping for shoes online is easy as long as you understand

Classic White

© photo by Positive Light Photography

- White satin shoes are available in all heel shapes and heights. Choose a shorter and wider heel for more comfort and stability if you're not typically fond of high heels

- Peep-toe shoes look great for summer weddings, and closed-toe shoes work best in the cold weather.

- Wear your heels around your house for at least thirty to sixty minutes prior to your wedding day to soften them up and get used to the way they feel.

Colorful

© photo by GH Kim Photography

- Find beautiful shoes that tie into your wedding color palette and add whimsical fun to your look.

- Colorful shoes can often be worn again, so you can get more mileage out of your purchase and enjoy the memories of your wedding day each time you wear them.

- If fabulous shoes are important to you, find a pair in navy, royal, baby blue, or turquoise and let them be your "something blue."

the return policies and are able to send back shoes that don't fit correctly or aren't quite what you are looking for.

If you find the shoes of your dreams but they pinch or rub in one particular area, visit a cobbler to find out if they can be stretched just enough to fix the problem. Cobblers can be miracle workers when it comes to shoe repair and maintenance.

Jeweled or Metallic

© photo by John and Joseph Photography

- Sparkling jeweled pumps and sandals can be coordinated with your jewelry and hair accessories for a whole new level of glamour and style.

- Make any shoe jeweled with shoe clips, vintage costume jewelry brooches, or clip-on earrings.

- Shoes made with metallic leathers and fabrics are a good middle ground if you don't want pure white or colorful shoes. They're modern and stylish in neutral tones that look great with all shades of white.

Flats

© photo by La Vie Photography

- If you never wear high heels in normal life, starting with your wedding can be quite uncomfortable. If you feel most confident and pretty in flats, go for it!

- To keep your look formal, stick with shoes made of satins, delicate fabrics, and sparkling embellishments instead of thicker leathers or canvas.

- Save your feet so you can celebrate all day long. Wear delicate-looking flats for your ceremony and change into heeled party shoes for your reception.

FASHION

115

JEWELRY

Sparkle and shine with jewels and accessories that accentuate your beauty

Women's love affair with beautiful jewelry is one that will last forever, and what better day to indulge in your passion for style than on your wedding day?

Classic jewelry is generally made from diamonds, pearls, or rhinestones in elegant shapes that bring to mind classic beauties like Grace Kelly, Audrey Hepburn, or Jacqueline Kennedy. Whether you choose something simple like a pair of diamond solitaire earrings and a single strand of pearls, or ultraglamorous chandelier earrings with layers of dramatic sparkling bracelets, a classic look is timeless.

Casual jewelry is often creatively made with freshwater pearls, semiprecious stones, beads, crystals, and metallic wire

Classic

© photo by Junebug Weddings

- Sparkling diamond or rhinestone jewelry like the bracelet and drop earrings shown above are timeless.

- A simple string of pearls evokes traditional elegance, while multiple strands paired with diamonds or rhinestones create a look of old Hollywood glamour.

- To keep rhinestone jewelry clean and tarnish free, store it in airtight plastic bags and keep it away from moisture or temperature changes.

- Pearls should be kept in a soft bag to prevent their being scratched and gently wiped clean with a damp cloth.

Casual

© photo by Junebug Weddings

- Freshwater pearls like the ones above come in many different colors, shapes, and sizes and create an elegant yet organic look.

- Semiprecious stones sparkle and shine for far less financial investment than diamond jewelry.

- Casual jewelry pieces can often be worn in everyday life as lovely reminders of your big day.

- There's no rule that says you can't mix and match your metals. Different shades of gold, silver, and bronze make a rich and shimmering metallic color palette.

or silk to create a look that's whimsical, playful, and pretty.

Alternative jewelry styles run the gamut from architecturally interesting, to bright, bold, and colorful and includes everything in between. Let your style shine through by choosing nontraditional jewelry that reflects the look you love.

Wearing vintage jewelry is a gorgeous way to add to your wedding day look. From the intricate filigree work of Edwardian times, to the dramatic angles of the art deco movement, to the more contemporary retro pieces, vintage jewelry adds history and personality that can't be beat.

Alternative

© photo by Junebug Weddings

- Play with the shape and scale of your jewelry for an alternative look. The round oversize beads in the necklace above look retro and fun, while clean, unembellished, angular lines look modern and chic.

- If the white of your wedding dress washes you out, wear a pop of rich color near your face in earrings or a necklace to brighten up your skin tone.

- Be sure colorful jewelry doesn't clash with the tones of your bridal bouquet or bridesmaids' dresses.

Vintage

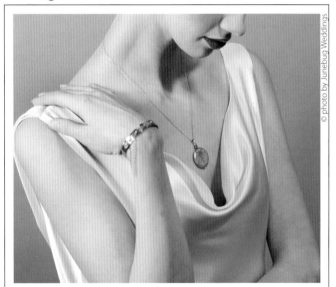

© photo by Junebug Weddings

- You don't have to go vintage from head to toe. Mix vintage jewelry with a modern dress or accessories for a fresh fashion statement that's just your style.

- Vintage jewelry is always a great ecofriendly fashion choice.

- Wearing jewelry that belonged to a beloved family member is a great way to keep her memory with you on your wedding day.

- Purchase vintage jewelry from a reputable and well-educated dealer so you can learn about what you're buying.

FASHION

RECEPTION STYLE

Fashion accents and accessories take your look from your ceremony to your celebration

Your wedding ceremony is a sacred event, but your reception is the time to party! Let the excitement of celebration come through in your fashion choices and "let your hair down" with fun changes to your look.

Wraps, capes, jackets, and sweaters are great accessories to have for your wedding, whether they're for practical purposes like traveling and staying protected from the elements or purely for fashion fun! Winter weddings call for luxurious, cozy cover-ups made of thick cashmere, fur, or faux fur, while spring and summer weddings call for just a light layer of silk or fine wool to add to your reception style.

In many cultures brides change their dresses numerous

Wraps, Capes, and Jackets

© photo by J. Garner Photography

- Cover your shoulders during your ceremony with a bolero like the one above and remove it for a new look at your reception.

- If you're traveling to a new location for your reception, make your grand entrance wearing your traveling cape or wrap.

- Have a simple cashmere shawl or wrap on hand for evening receptions in case the weather cools down.

- For more casual weddings, slip a classic fitted cashmere cardigan over your dress to fend off the evening chill.

Dress Change

© photo by Yours by John Photography

- If incorporating your family's cultural traditions is an important part of your day, enjoy the best of both worlds and wear traditional garb for your ceremony and a modern white wedding dress for your reception.

- Change into a shorter-length party dress once the

- traditional reception events are done and the dance party begins so you can comfortably celebrate late into the night.

- If fashion is your thing, change into a reception dress for no other reason than fashion fun!

times throughout the celebration to signify different important values, virtues, and symbols of luck. You can pull from this tradition for whatever reason you choose and make the most of this great fashion opportunity.

Hairstyle and accessory changes make a big visual impact and are easy to do if you organize ahead of time. Swap out your veil for a more lighthearted hair accessory at the same time you change your hairstyle, and slip into alternative accessories before heading into your reception to delight your guests with your fashion-savvy style.

Hairstyle Change

© photo by La Vie Photography

- Take down that traditional updo and let your locks flow for a more party-appropriate style.

- If you want your hair swept up but a bit more casual, try a neat and playful ponytail.

- If your stylist can't stay until your reception, have him or her teach you and your bridesmaids how to change your hairstyle from one look to the other.

- Have extra hairpins, tools, and styling products handy to make the transition easy.

Accessory Change

© photo by GH Kim Photography

- Remove your veil and wear a dramatic hair accessory instead for ease of movement and additional style.

- If you wear white flowers in your hair for your ceremony, try freshening up and changing to colorful flowers for your party.

- Break out your dancing shoes! Change into pretty flats if your feet are tired or into more dramatic colorful or jeweled evening shoes for added party flair.

- Carry a pretty handbag to your reception with all your essentials inside.

FASHION

YOUR MAID OF HONOR

She's your cheerleader, your fashion consultant, your surrogate hostess, and your friend

Choosing your maid of honor (MOH) can be a sweet and challenging experience. Ideally you want to choose someone whom you love and trust who has enough time and energy to support you throughout your entire planning process. To make sure both you and your MOH are happy with your choice, start off by being clear about what you're requesting.

Give her a wish list of things you anticipate needing her help with and give her time to consider it before signing on.

Traditionally your MOH will help you pick out your dress and the fashions for the whole bridal party. She'll make sure that the bridesmaids attend their fittings and arrive at the altar looking put together from head to toe.

The One You Turn To

© photo by La Vie Photography

- Who's always in your corner? Who reminds you to never put yourself down? Who makes you feel better when you're around her? Chances are whoever that is, she's the perfect choice to be your maid of honor.

- Blessed with sisters and friends who all fit the bill?

- Choose your oldest sister first or the friend you've known the longest. That decision will be easy to justify should hurt feelings arise.

- Choose out of love, not out of guilt.

Before Your Wedding

© photo by GH Kim Photography

- In addition to having her lend a hand as a fashion consultant before your wedding, ask your MOH to stay close by on your wedding day to help put on your dress, touch up your makeup, and bustle your gown.

- It's customary for your MOH to pay for her dress, your bridal shower or bachelorette party, and a wedding gift. Keep her resources in mind and don't expect her to go out of her comfort zone financially unless you're planning on contributing.

Before your wedding she'll be the hostess of your bridal shower and your bachelorette party, and she'll help you keep track of all the thoughtful gifts you receive. She'll spread the word on everything from where you're registered to what time to arrive at your rehearsal dinner, and she'll help you make dozens of important decisions along the way.

When your big day comes, she'll be there to take your calls, walk down the aisle in front of you, sign your license, and act as your backup hostess when necessary.

YELLOW LIGHT

Your MOH is there to lend her support throughout your wedding planning process. While it's thoughtful for her to give you extra time and patience for being the bride, don't forget what's going on in her life. Be supportive of her and you'll stay friends long after your wedding day.

During Your Ceremony

© photo by La Vie Photography

- Your MOH will stand to the right of you, holding his ring and your bouquet during your ceremony.

- If your train or veil needs straightening, your MOH will attend to it before she takes your bouquet.

- Once your license is signed, your MOH will ensure that all your personal items are transferred from the ceremony to your reception. Then she'll arrive ahead of you to alert your venue to prepare for your grand entrance.

At Your Reception

© photo by GH Kim Photography

- It's common practice, but not required, that your MOH give a toast at your reception. You may also call on her to dance with your groom and his father and to gather the single women together for the toss of your bouquet.

- People will naturally gravitate toward your MOH and best man to ask questions. Be sure they know all the relevant info your guests need, from where to have their parking validated to the location of the restrooms.

YOUR BEST MAN

He's your go-to guy from your bachelor party to your bon voyage

Choosing a stand-up guy to stand up for you does require some forethought. You'll want someone who you really like and trust, someone who's reliable, knows what's important to you, and has enough time to have your back all the way to your honeymoon.

Your best man will plan your much-anticipated bachelor party, and he'll coordinate with your maid of honor to make sure that your entire bridal party has the information they need about important events like your rehearsal. He'll come with you to pick out your tuxes and help you put together your look, and if you're lucky, he'll have some great advice on what's in style and what can help you stand out from the rest of the guys.

On your wedding day, your best man will be at your side to

Your Go-To Guy

© photo by Positive Light Photography

- Your best friend or your oldest brother is an obvious first choice to be your best man.

- Give your best man a list of the jobs you need help with when you ask him to take on the role.

- Traditionally, your best man will pay for his tux rental, your bachelor party, and a wedding gift. If you want your best man to pay for additional items, let him know when you ask him to step in.

Before Your Wedding

© photo by Yours by John Photography

- Throughout the planning process your best man will be there to be sure your groomsmen work as a team.

- Your best man will attend fittings with you and the guys, and if he's extra-organized, he'll show up at the wedding with shoe polish, extra socks, and a sewing kit.

- If a traditional raucous bachelor party is not your style, be sure your best man knows it before he makes plans.

- Turn to Chapter 19 for creative bachelor party ideas.

122

take your calls and to be sure that your groomsmen show up on time and on task, perfectly dressed to impress. He'll hold your bride's ring for you during your ceremony, stand next to you while you say your vows, and make the whole thing official by signing your license as a witness.

When the party portion of your day gets underway, your best man will kick off your celebration by raising a glass to you and your bride. He'll dance with your new wife after you and her father do. And, when your wedding day comes to a close, he'll be there to drive you to the airport, take your gifts to your house, and return your tuxes if necessary.

With all the tasks required, being a best man is a true honor and a real responsibility. Remember to thank him for accepting the job and for everything he does for you along the way.

During Your Ceremony

© photo by GH Kim Photography

- Signing your marriage license and having her ring at the ready are two of the most important roles your best man will play.

- During your ceremony, your best man will stand to the left of you at the altar, and he'll be seated to the left of you at your reception table.

- Give your best man an envelope with any payments still owed to your vendors. Ask him to pass them out for you and to keep the receipts until after your honeymoon.

At Your Reception

© photo by Yours by John Photography

- Ask your best man to say a toast for you and your bride that is one to three minutes in length.

- If you're at all concerned about what he might share, ask him to omit personal stories and jokes and focus on what he wishes for your marriage.

- If he's single and naturally sociable, ask him to help keep the single ladies in your bridal party and family dancing so you can focus on your bride.

YOUR SUPPORTING CAST

Friends and family get in the act to create a picture-perfect wedding

Choosing your bridal party and contributors to your wedding ceremony provides a fantastic opportunity to honor your friends and family. If you're having a large wedding, there will be plenty of spots for bridesmaids and groomsmen. If you're having a small intimate affair, you'll still need to choose ushers and others to contribute readings or music to your ceremony.

For your bridal party you'll want people whom you love to hang out with and who enjoy one another's company. After all, you'll all be together for your shower, your rehearsal dinner, and your wedding, at the very least. Choose people who are enthusiastic about your engagement and who have the available time to attend necessary fittings and functions. For

Your Bridal Party

© photo by J. Garner Photography

- A couple's closest friends and siblings usually compose the bridal party. There are generally two to ten bridesmaids and groomsmen.

- While it's conventional, it's not necessary that you have the same number of attendants on each side or that his side be all guys, or your side be all girls.

- Traditionally the members of your bridal party pay for their outfits, wedding gifts, and their lodging if necessary, and they should be on hand to support you throughout your planning process.

Attendants and Helpful Friends

© photo by La Vie Photography

- Ushers are typically male and have the important job of seating guests and escorting mothers down the aisle last. The lucky mother of the bride pictured above has both of her handsome sons at her side.

- Traditionally your ushers will need to pay for their outfits and attend your rehearsal dinner.

- Teenagers are ideal as ushers. The role gives them something important to do, without requiring too much time or other commitment from them.

your ushers choose responsible friends and family members who are usually punctual and polite.

For your ceremony you may have special readings, poems, or songs that you would like to share with your guests, which is a perfect way to ask family members to participate. Want to add an extra splash of sweetness and light to your ceremony? Then get the little ones involved. There's really nothing cuter than a little boy in a tuxedo or a little girl throwing petals as she makes her way down the aisle.

ZOOM

If your beloved pet is a member of your wedding party, you're not alone. Increasing numbers of couples are including their pets in their ceremonies, and sales of doggie tuxedos and ring pillows from pet stores have soared. While pets are adorable, you will want to consider the obvious risks when making this decision.

Flower Girls and Ring Bearers

© photo by GH Kim Photography

- To give little ones extra confidence, have them walk down the aisle together. Having a buddy can help calm last-minute jitters.

- Typically children four to eight years old fill these special roles.

- Kids who are naturally outgoing and truly excited to participate have a better chance of fulfilling their tasks well on your wedding day.

- Seating parents in an aisle seat where kids can easily see them also helps them feel safer.

Man's Best Friend

© photo by La Vie Photography

- Dogs are the most popular pets to include in weddings because they are the easiest to train.

- If you decide to include your pet, have someone designated to take care of him or her throughout the day.

- Musician Gwen Stefani had her sheepdog, Winston, escort her down the aisle. Actor Adam Sandler had his dog, Meatball, as his best man.

- For more information about fashion options for your pets, visit our Resources section.

STYLE FOR THE GIRLS
Your wedding: the ultimate dress-up party for fashionable friends

The colors, shapes, fabrics, and details of your bridesmaids' fashion will make a huge impact on your overall wedding style, so have fun coming up with their looks and creating the wedding style you're dreaming of.

Many classic and casual dresses will be available from a single bridesmaid's dress designer or boutique. If you're in charge of ordering the dresses for each of your girlfriends,

have them try on the store's sample dresses to choose the best size. If they are out of town, get their bust, waist, hip, and waist-to-floor measurements, as well as their regular dress and bra sizes, to give to your dress salesperson. If the correct size is in question, opt for the larger one. It's always easier to take a dress in than to let one out. Alterations will probably be necessary for a proper fit and hem length, so

Classic Style

© photo by Positive Light Photography

- Full-length dresses, like the ones shown above, are the most formal choice for bridesmaids and look elegant and timeless at black-tie weddings.

- Matching dresses in the same shape and color make a dramatic impact, especially with large wedding parties.

- Look for dresses in fabrics like silk taffeta, charmeuse, organza, or chiffon for the most classic look.

- Shoes should match the color of the dress or be a sparkling metallic or jeweled shoe with a mid-heel or high heel.

Casual Style

© photo by La Vie Photography

- Let your bridesmaids choose their own neckline and dress shape from a selection of dresses made from the same fabric. You'll get a uniform look with some fun variety, and your maids will feel superconfident in their favorite style.

- Tea-length dresses add a playful quality to the wedding party look and can show off newsworthy shoes.

- Fabrics can have slight patterns or textures within their weave or be made of casual materials like cotton or linen.

be sure the dresses arrive in plenty of time to be finalized without a rush.

Bridesmaids traditionally pay for their own dresses and accessories, so be conscientious of what you're asking of them financially, especially if they are also traveling to attend your wedding or hosting parties in your honor. If you have your heart set on a dress that is above their budget range, meet them halfway and contribute to the cost.

The dresses are only one part of your bridal party's look. Shoes, jewelry, purses, flowers, hair accessories, and other stylish extras are all up for your unique interpretation and give you a chance to explore your fashion vision. Choose luxe gold shoes for a glamorous modern affair, fresh flowers for their hair at your seaside beach wedding, or a sparkling art deco rhinestone brooch for their necklines at your vintage-inspired soiree.

Alternative Style

© photo by La Vie Photography

- Want to include a guy on your side of the wedding party? Give him a shirt, tie, pocket square, or other accessory to coordinate his fashion with the ladies'.

- Give your bridesmaids an idea of the level of formality you're looking for and color swatches of your wedding color palette, and then send them off shopping for a unique dress that's all their own.

- Choose an array of tones for the bridesmaids' dresses and create a multicolor effect.

Fun Extras

© photo by Positive Light Photography

- Honor your MOH by styling her to stand out from the rest with a special dress, sash, fresh-flower corsage, or brooch like the one above.

- Shoes can be the focus instead of the accessory. Choose simple little black dresses for your bridesmaids and brightly colored shoes that steal the show.

- Give your gals a little guidance as to the style of jewelry you would like them to wear. The right jewels can easily dress up or dress down a simple gown.

STYLE FOR THE GUYS
Suit up your entourage in fashion that complements your style

There's nothing like a group of well-dressed men to make a big fashion impact. The styles you choose for your groomsmen will add personality to the overall wedding style and help define the level of formality of your event. Classic suits and tuxedos say romance and sophistication, modern suits with creative accents express fashion-forward style, and alternative attire like kilts shout creativity.

If you and your wedding party are renting suits or tuxes, come up with a game plan for how to get everyone fitted. If some of your guys are out of town, consider renting from a national chain so they can arrange their rental from their own hometown. If you want to work with a local shop, find out exactly which measurements they require to determine each man's size and have your friends visit a professional tailor to

Classic Style

- Classic tuxes look best if every member of your wedding party is coordinating their details. Rent from the same resource or tell your guys what lapel shape, tie size, vest, or cummerbund fabric to look for.

- Whatever kind of tux you're wearing, your groomsmen should follow suit with the same style and color.

- Bring extra cuff links, studs, ties, and pocket squares in case someone's goes missing.

- A lint roller works wonders to clean up dark suit fabric.

Casual Style

- Ask each groomsman to wear a black or dark gray suit, then add color or interest with their shirts, ties, pocket squares, and boutonnieres.

- Many tuxedo rental shops also rent suits. Visit a few in your area to see their selections.

- If your guys are scattered across the country, find their shirts and ties in an Internet shop and send them a link so they can purchase online.

- Specify if they will need shirts with French cuffs for cuff links.

have their measurements taken correctly.

If you would like your wedding party to purchase matching suits, let them know well in advance since fittings and alterations can take time and they may have to save up some funds. Nice suits can be big investments, so be considerate with your financial expectations and think about pitching in to help with costs if appropriate.

Alternative Style

© photo by John and Joseph Photography

- At ultracasual celebrations like the beach wedding above, your groomsmen don't have to wear suits just because you are. As long as they coordinate, you'll all look great.

- If you wear a military uniform, your guys will look great in coordinating tuxedos or dark suits.

- Your whole wedding party doesn't need to be Scottish to wear kilts with their formal wear. If it's a look you love, go for it and get one for each of your guys.

Fun Extras

© photo by John and Joseph Photography

- Choose wild ties for your groomsmen and give them to your guys as gifts.

- If you all wear something truly out of the ordinary, like sneakers with your suits, surprise socks, or unusual matching cuff links, don't forget to capture them on film.

- At a Hawaiian beach wedding, groomsmen look handsome in traditional kukui nut necklaces instead of boutonnieres.

- Mixing and matching colors and patterns can create a sophisticated and dapper look.

GIFTS & GRATITUDE

Show your appreciation and celebrate your relationships with thoughtful notes and gifts

The members of your wedding party are your friends, your family, your support systems, and your comic relief. They've no doubt played important roles in your lives, and throughout your wedding planning, they will shower you with sweet gifts and gestures, so it is only natural for you to reciprocate. Showing gratitude for all they've done is important.

Coming up with thank-you gifts that express what your friends mean to you can be a superfun and creative project. What does each of your friends love to do? Show them how well you know them with personalized gifts: a specialty single malt scotch for the connoisseur, a dinner out at a new local restaurant for the foodie, tickets to a ball game for the sports

Fun Events

© photo by La Vie Photography

- Say thanks by treating your wedding party to an activity you want to do together in the days before or on the day of your wedding.

- Spring for all the guys to play nine holes of golf, eat a great brunch, or get

hot shaves at the barbershop the morning of the wedding.

- Spring for all the girls to get pedicures, get their horoscopes read, or have their makeup done on the big day.

Gifts for Your Guys

© photo by Junebug Weddings

- Sterling silver gifts like cuff links, flasks, key chains, Swiss army knives, or money clips are classic and elegant ways to say thank you.

- Find each groomsman a pair of vintage cuff links that matches his personal-

ity and hobbies. Scour thrift stores and Internet auction sites for great selections.

- Each gift doesn't have to be the same. Your friends are all different, so play to their personalities to find the perfect thank-you gifts you know they'll love.

nut, a first-edition book for the scholar, fabulous accessories for the dedicated follower of fashion, or activities you can do together for friends who love to get up and go.

While thoughtful gifts are always appreciated, nothing says thank you like publicly declaring your gratitude, so raise a glass to those who have shaped your life and made your wedding possible. A little recognition goes a long way to honor those you love.

ZOOM

Thank-you gifts don't have to be expensive; it truly is the thought that counts. No matter what gift you give, accompany it with a card and a message from the heart. Tell the members of your wedding party what their friendship means to you and why you're grateful they're part of your big day.

Gifts for Your Girls

© photo by One Thousand Words Photography

- Jewelry to wear on the wedding day is always a welcome gift. Be sure to let them know ahead of time that you've got their jewelry covered.

- Classic jewelry they can wear for years will remind them of your friendship. Engrave it with a sweet sentiment to make it more personal.

- Personal stationery customized with their monogram, initials, or another pretty design will never go out of style.

- Give them something pampering they wouldn't normally buy for themselves.

Saying Thanks

© photo by La Vie Photography

- Give a short thank-you speech at your reception, introducing your wedding party and explaining what makes each of them important parts of your lives.

- The rehearsal dinner is a great time to give out thank-you gifts to the wedding party and family since it will be a gathering just for you and them.

- Wedding planning is full of small details. Don't let the little things people do for you go unnoticed; small gestures can make a huge impact.

TRADITIONAL RESPONSIBILITIES

Time-honored customs welcome family members to participate in your wedding planning process

Your engagement is bound to spark a flurry of excitement and expectations from you, your friends, and your family. Even if you haven't been thinking about your wedding since your were little, chances are one or both of your parents have, and even the friends closest to you may have preconceived notions of how your wedding will unfold.

To help you navigate the waters between your desires and those of your loved ones, here is a rundown of the traditional family member responsibilities that are often the center of people's expectations (whether they know it or not). These are merely guidelines that are meant to be tailored to the resources and realities of your unique relationships and families.

The Bride's Family

© photo by J. Garner Photography

- Sit down with your fiancé and both sets of parents to discuss their top three expectations for your wedding. Consider how these requests might fit in with your vision.

- Traditionally your dad will walk you down the aisle, make a toast at your reception, and dance with you after your first dance.

- Your mom will be there to help you get ready, dance with your groom, and be a gracious hostess at your reception.

The Groom's Family

© photo by GH Kim Photography

- Traditional roles may leave the groom's family feeling left out of the wedding planning. Be sure they have an opportunity to contribute and share their wishes.

- The rehearsal dinner gives the groom's family a chance to show their gratitude and excitement about your marriage. Take their desires and resources to heart when planning this special event.

- Honor the groom's family by making sure your photographer covers them thoroughly and takes any special portraits or additional photos they would like.

Traditionally the bride's parents pay for the lion's share of their daughter's wedding, including the engagement party, the dress and veil, all of the expenses related to the ceremony including music, and all of the expenses, for the reception except for the beverages (which the groom's family may cover). In addition they'll pay for transportation and your engagement announcement in the newspaper.

The groom's parents are commonly responsible for the rehearsal dinner, a wedding gift (often a monetary contribution), the beverages for the reception, and their own wedding attire.

Keep in mind that your parents may not be able to financially support your wedding planning expectations. Traditional norms have changed rapidly over the years, and now almost 50 percent of couples pay for their wedding themselves. Communicate clearly so everyone, including you, knows what to expect financially.

Communicate

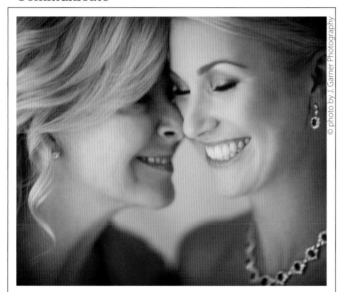

© photo by J. Garner Photography

- Family members will appreciate a schedule of events for your wedding weekend well in advance so they can plan for parties, pictures, and special events.

- Pay close attention to time frames and transportation so people can easily get where you need them to be.

- Start your own wedding Web site to keep people in the loop as details unfold. Sharing in your process will create a lasting sense of connection.

Delegate

© photo by GH Kim Photography

- You'll need more than financial support from your families to pull off a great wedding. If you're paying for your wedding yourself, enlist the help of your relatives in other areas.

- Consider sending out a contact list of all participating members so they can coordinate with one another and plan surprises.

- A lot of people really want to help, but they can't read your mind. This is one time it is absolutely acceptable to ask for huge favors. Don't be shy!

133

HONORING THOSE YOU LOVE

Shower your family and friends with love by offering them a special role in your big day

One of the best ways to make your wedding special is to honor the people closest to you and ask them to show off their unique talents and personalities. No doubt you have friends and family members who are artists, chefs, musicians, singers, or just great public speakers who would love to contribute to your wedding. Think about the passions and hobbies of those closest to you and get creative with them about the ways they can contribute.

For your ceremony choose inspirational people from your life as candle lighters, ushers, readers, and performers or have someone you mutually admire act as your officiant. Enlist creative people to help decorate and design your ceremonial

Play Up Passions

© photo by La Vie Photography

- Friends and family members don't have to be accomplished musicians to bring a sweet note to your day.

- Think outside the box. Get your friend who's a painter to capture your day on canvas, inspire your girls to do a cancan dance for your groom, or have the groomsmen sing a cappella.

- Rent a luxury tour bus and have your city-wise cousin take your guests on a local adventure before your rehearsal.

During the Ceremony

© photo by GH Kim Photography

- Asking your mothers to light the candelabras or unity candles at your ceremony is a lovely way to get them involved.

- Have a favorite passage or poem that symbolizes your union? Ask your sister to give an impassioned reading, or have her write one of her own.

- To honor your parents, add the presentation of a single flower and heartfelt thanks to them at the opening of your ceremony.

space. Have your uncle build you a floral arbor or have your aunt who's an artist create your program. For your reception look for people with unique skills to help make your party exceptional. Have your mom decorate your cake, your brother's band play your first dance song, or your friend make a video of the two of you.

No matter how you choose to honor your loved ones, their contributions will emphasize the coming together of your two families and two communities, which is at the core of what weddings have always been about.

YELLOW ● LIGHT

Don't forget to order corsages and boutonnieres for parents and grandparents and to make special seating arrangements for family members at your ceremony and reception. When it comes to making people feel loved and appreciated, it's often the little things that make the biggest difference.

During the Reception

© photo by La Vie Photography

- Dancing with your dad right after your first dance with your husband is a sweet way to honor his special place in your life. If you have a special stepfather as well, dance with him next.

- Asking people to share a toast during your reception is a simple way to include them.

- Public speaking is a real fear for many people. Don't take it personally if a friend or family member declines to speak up at your wedding.

In Memoriam

© photo by La Vie Photography

- The honoring of ancestors is a central feature of wedding rituals around the world. Create your own special way to pay tribute to those who laid the foundation for your future.

- Add a photograph to your bouquet or design a memorial on your guest book table to bring the presence of someone you love and miss to your wedding day.

- Carry a symbol of remembrance such as a piece of lace from your grandmother's dress or an antique watch from your great-grandfather.

135

FASHION FOR MOMS
Fabulous fashions for your mothers and grandmothers

Modern mothers of the bride and groom have many choices when it comes to their wedding fashion. The ultratraditional rules from years ago are gone, so most mothers now opt for dresses and accessories that truly represent their own personal style as well as coordinate nicely with the style and formality of the day.

To be sure your mothers feel confident with their choices, it's smart to let them know if you have preferences for the styles they choose or to make it a project you can work on together. Shopping with your mother or future mother-in-law can give her the chance to easily follow your lead and learn which options you think will best complement the style of the event.

Traditionally the mother of the groom defers to the mother

Classic

© photo by Positive Light Photography

- With a sleeveless dress, a matching bolero jacket like the one shown above will show respect during a traditional ceremony and warm bare arms later in the evening.

- Full-length dresses are appropriate for formal events at any time of day.

- For a daytime event, the dress should stay simple and sophisticated without extra embellishment.

- For an elegant evening celebration, glamorous jewelry and accessories or a gown with more intricate detailing can liven up a look.

Casual

© photo by Positive Light Photography

- A cocktail-length dress is perfect for most casual weddings and can be dressed up or dressed down with fresh flowers, shoes, jewelry, a purse, and other accessories.

- Items from a favorite designer are more likely to be worn again for other special occasions.

- The style of the wedding, venue, the time of year, and the theme of the wedding can all inspire the fashion choices of your mothers and grandmothers.

of the bride when it comes to choosing the appropriate fashion for the wedding. At the very least the moms should communicate about the dresses they are planning to wear so their styles won't compete but will look gorgeous together. There will most likely be important family photos with both sides of the family together, so similar colors and levels of formality for the mothers will look best. Their outfits should also complement the colors and styles of the rest of the wedding party.

Moms should enjoy this opportunity to have fun with fashion and embrace their roles as honored guests of the day.

Whether it's a custom-made formal gown, a simple black cocktail dress, or a playful outfit for a casual affair, your mothers' looks should be age appropriate but not matronly. They should give themselves lots of time to find the perfect dress and choose something that makes them feel beautiful, confident, and special.

Alternative

© photo by GH Kim Photography

- Moms can have fun with wedding themes, too. Fun colors and accessories are the easiest ways to turn a classic look into a thematic look without going over the top.

- At a beach wedding, a flowing lightweight summer dress will be the most comfortable. If it's a winter wonderland theme, look for fabric and accessories with a sparkling metallic sheen.

- Even if the bride isn't wearing a traditional dress, no one, including the mothers, should wear white to the wedding.

Fun Extras

© photo by La Vie Photography

- If your mothers will be wearing pinned-on corsages, they should be informed so they can choose their dress fabric and bodice shape accordingly.

- Hats can be fabulous fashion accessories for events like weddings. They should be tried on with the dress ahead of time and taken to the hairstylist on the day of the wedding.

- Family heirloom jewelry and accessories lend a bit of romance and history to the wedding day and honor those who came before.

FASHION FOR DADS
Fabulous fashion for your fathers and grandfathers

The roles of fathers evolve as their children grow up, but no matter how much things change, one thing is certain: Your wedding will be a big day for them. Honoring their importance in your wedding planning is a great thing to remember, and even small details like their wedding day fashion can work wonders to make them feel like the special family members they are.

Most dads play an important role in the wedding itself—walking you down the aisle, acting as host, giving a speech, or greeting family and friends—so their attire should fit in with the look of the event and make them feel fantastic while they're in the spotlight. Tell them what the rest of the men in the wedding party will be wearing and what you envision for them. If they're uncomfortable in formal wear, or even if

Classic

© photo by GH Kim Photography

- If the men in the wedding party are wearing tuxedos, the fathers should wear them as well.

- Dads can update a classic tuxedo they already own with a new shirt, tie, shoes, and other accessories.

- The fathers' tuxedos can be rented along with the rest of the groomsmen's so they will be the same or nicely coordinating.

- Communicate with both fathers early on about what they will be expected to wear so they have plenty of time to prepare.

Casual

© photo by GH Kim Photography

- If the men in the wedding party are wearing dark formal suits, the fathers should wear them, too.

- Next to the groom and groomsmen, the fathers should be the most dressed up men at the event.

- Casual suits come in many colors—navy, tan, light gray, dark gray, or patterned—and many dads already own at least one.

- The father of the bride and father of the groom should check in to be sure their casual looks are harmonious.

they're really excited about it, you can offer to go shopping and work on it with them. If the groom and groomsmen are all renting tuxedos, inviting your dads along for fittings can help get them involved, make them feel welcome, and give them confidence that their look will be exactly right.

MAKE IT EASY

Is there something special your dad wore to his own wedding that would still look great today? Whether it's his handkerchief or his cuff links, it's the little mementos like that, full of charm and emotion, that can start a family tradition of your own.

Alternative

© photo by Yours by John Photography

- If the groomsmen are wearing something truly unique, like the kilts shown above, give the same outfit or accessories to the fathers to tie the family's look to the wedding party's.

- For any alternatively styled wedding, the fathers should be given a little fashion guidance so they'll feel like they fit in on the big day.

- If the father of the groom is in the wedding party, be sure the father of the bride's outfit coordinates or is given equal thought and attention.

Fun Extras

© photo by Positive Light Photography

- Family heirloom accessories like a pocket watch or cuff links are a great addition to a father's wedding day style.

- Dads can wear a pocket square or tie that corresponds with the colors of the wedding party so they look like part of the gang.

- Special boutonnieres for the dads and grandfathers will honor their importance and show off their position in the family to guests who haven't yet met them.

139

FASHION FOR KIDS & ATTENDANTS

Explore some fabulous fashions for flower girls, ring bearers, and attendants

Having children in your wedding party can add joy and sweetness to your day and be a great way to honor the little ones you love. When choosing fashion for young children, comfort is key and each child has a different level of tolerance when it comes to clothing. Communicate with their parents about the clothing they normally gravitate toward and how they have done in the past with dress-up situations. Choose items you think they'll enjoy wearing and schedule the day so that they don't have to be in formal wear for too many long hours before the ceremony and reception.

For older children, make the experience of being part of your wedding extra special by involving them in picking

Flower Girls

© photo by La Vie Photography

- Choose dresses that are pretty but comfortable so they will fully enjoy the experience. Look for soft fabrics and trims, and bodices, necks, and armholes that aren't too tight.

- Add a dash of your wedding colors with a sash or ribbons for their hair.

- If they're carrying a basket with flower petals down the aisle, give it to them early with extra petals so they can practice and play.

Ring Bearer

© photo by GH Kim Photography

- A suit or tuxedo matching the men in the wedding party will always look sharp. Many tuxedo rental shops also carry children's sizes.

- Give him a boutonniere or other accessory that's just like the big boys' in the wedding party.

- Traditional ring bearer outfits with knickers, shirts, and vests have a classic, romantic charm and come in colors to match your wedding color palette.

- Choose a ring pillow or other ring box that's easy for a little one to carry.

out their outfits. Spend a little time with them and let them choose from a couple of options that would both look wonderful, or let them decide on some of their accessories. Just the time spent with you and your partner will make their experience that much richer.

For junior bridesmaids and ushers, choose styles that will coordinate well with the rest of the wedding party so they'll look and feel like part of the group. When planning each outfit, think of how everyone will look together in a large group portrait.

Teenagers and preteens in your wedding party will probably be organizing their own clothing for your wedding day but may not have much experience with dressing up for formal occasions. Give them a checklist a few weeks ahead of time of the clothing and accessories they should be sure to bring along.

Junior Bridesmaids

© photo by La Vie Photography

- Junior bridesmaids are older than flower girls but younger than bridesmaids, so choose age-appropriate dresses they'll feel comfortable but still fancy in.

- Choose dresses in a shape or color similar to the bridesmaids', but give them a slight variation so they stand out as their own important group.

- A special gift, like jewelry to wear on the wedding day, will add to their look and be a sweet treat for a young girl.

Ushers and Attendants

© photo by J. Garner Photography

- At a formal wedding the ushers and other attendants should wear the same tuxedos or suits as the rest of the wedding party, with a stylish variation in their accessories. Different boutonnieres, ties, pocket squares, or vests will differentiate them from the groomsmen.

- At a casual wedding ushers and attendants don't have to be as dressed up as the groomsmen, but they should coordinate with one another in some way so they can be identified as honored members of the wedding party.

GIFTS & REGISTRIES

Choose the gifts you'll love to own as you begin your future together

Registering for all those wonderful wedding gifts is a perk of being soon-to-be marrieds and is a helpful guide to your family and friends who want to congratulate you on your new life together.

Work together to choose items in every price range that you are confident you'll love to own, and register soon after you announce your engagement for all of those prewedding events. Stay focused on the kinds of things that will really fit in with your lifestyle, and try not to get tempted or overwhelmed by all the options.

That said, you should try to have fun with it, too. These days all kinds of stores have wedding registries, and there are numerous gift registry Web sites that allow you to choose items from any online shop. You can even register for help

Home Decor

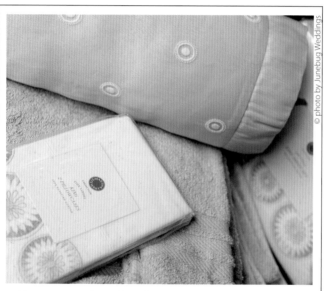

© photo by Junebug Weddings

- Monogrammed towels and sheets are classic wedding gifts that never go out of style and can be made with old-fashioned or modern lettering.

- Picture frames come in handy after a wedding for all of your beautiful wedding photos.

- New luggage in different sizes makes a great gift, and you'll use it and appreciate it for years to come.

- Balance big-ticket items for your home with less-expensive options like basic linens, decor accessories, or small electronics.

In the Kitchen

© photo by Junebug Weddings

- If you love to cook, register for fun and useful kitchen tools and utensils as well as various cookbooks.

- Mixers, blenders, and other small appliances can be handy yet affordable gifts.

- Registering for a formal china pattern is the most classic registry item and makes a wonderful family heirloom.

- Check each store's return policy before you begin your registry so you will know what to do if you don't receive full sets of things like china, silverware, or glassware.

with your honeymoon or fun activities like dinner out on the town, French lessons, or couple's cooking classes. See the Resources section for information on popular online registries of all kinds.

Etiquette states that you should never include your registry information in your wedding invitation. Have your parents, maid of honor, and best man spread the word, include it in invitations to other events like wedding showers and engagement parties, or list it on your wedding Web site.

Follow Your Interests

© photo by La Vie Photography

- Specialty foods and wines are perfect gifts for food aficionados and couples building their wine collection. Register for a food or wine of the month club.

- Let your hobbies guide your unorthodox registry items. Register for activities on your honeymoon like

spa treatments, romantic dinners, or helicopter rides.

- Outdoor gear and athletic stores offer registries to help you on your next hiking, hunting, or camping trip.

- Build your music library by registering for new CDs or music downloads.

Charitable Giving

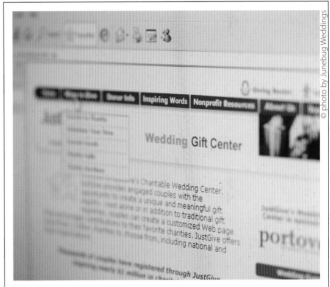

© photo by Junebug Weddings

- If you already own enough essentials for your home, choose a charity that's close to your heart and ask guests to make a donation in lieu of wedding gifts.

- Register with stores that partner with charitable organizations so that part

of the proceeds from your gift sales will benefit those in need.

- Give guests the option of a traditional gift or a charitable gift, as some people will be excited to buy something special just for you.

CLASSIC PHOTOGRAPHY
Traditional wedding photography techniques create heirloom images that last a lifetime

When your wedding is long over, your pictures will remain to remind you of your big day and the important people who shared it with you, so schedule some time in your day for classic photography that focuses on families and the two of you together.

While traditional photography has given way to photo-journalism over the last few decades, today's classic photos are a new kind of gorgeous, and traditional arrangements are still expected by most members of your parents' and grand-parents' generations. If you have a large family, your wedding may provide a rare opportunity to get everyone together for a complete family photo. What an excellent time to also get

Couple's Portrait

© photo by J. Garner Photography

- When you're having your picture taken, have fun, relax, and breathe. You'll feel better and look better.

- Your favorite wedding portraits are priceless, so be sure you have copies made of them. Store them in an archival box between sheets of acid-free paper.

- If you feel uncomfortable in front of the camera but you want a classic portrait, let your photographer know. He or she should have lots of ways to put you at ease.

Family Photos

© photo by La Vie Photography

- A well-posed shot doesn't mean boring. A good photographer connects with people and creates photos with personality.

- Chances are your family portrait is the one you'll still have hanging on your wall when you celebrate your golden anniversary.

- To create your family photo list, write down your immediate family members and grandparents first. Talk to your photographer about the time necessary for those photos, and then add other family members according to your schedule.

beautiful portraits of your parents and grandparents, and what a beautiful way to show them how much they mean to you.

In addition to capturing people, classic photography also captures places, from country meadows to urban cathedrals, from beautiful ballrooms to family backyards. After all, where you choose to have your wedding is important to you and is bound to become more so once you're married. A great wedding photographer will be able to create artistic classic photos of the people and places that made your wedding special and provide you with heirloom images you'll treasure.

PHOTOS & VIDEO

Bridal Party Photos

© photo by J. Garner Photography

- Here's where classic portraiture gets really creative! Photographers feel more inclined to be playful when they're taking photos of your bridal party.

- As you're having your photo taken throughout the day, stand up straight and smile, but don't hold your breath or lock your knees.

- Be sure to let your photographer know if you want individual portraits with members of your bridal party, and then factor those into your schedule.

Landscape and Architectural Photography

© photo by J. Garner Photography

- Landscape and architectural photography add yet another dimension to classic wedding photos.

- Large backdrops like territorial views and landmarks, and small backdrops like stairways and bridges, set the stage for classic portraits.

- It's become commonplace for photographers to take photos of couples in various locations prior to their wedding and during the time between their ceremony and reception. Let your photographer know if you have some special spots where you would like to stop for photos along the way.

PHOTOJOURNALISM

Spontaneous photography captures emotional moments and artfully documents your wedding

Photojournalistic wedding photography tells the story of your wedding day and allows you to see through a lens why there is nothing more beautiful than real life and real relationships. After all, what could be more precious than your dad crying, your grandma groovin', or your getaway car being decorated with tin cans and pink polka dots?

An outstanding photojournalistic photographer understands how important your special moments are and captures them for you to keep for the rest of your life.

As part of their photography package, most photojournalists will begin shooting while you're getting ready, to capture the anticipation and beauty of your transformation into a

Getting Ready Shots

© photo by La Vie Photography

- Some of the most special photos of your day will be taken when you put on your dress and see yourself as a bride for the first time. Don't rush this moment!

- If you have a photography team, or enough extra time, get coverage of the guys getting ready as well.

- Let your photographer know if there is anything you don't want photographed. Authentic photojournalism doesn't have to include pictures of you in your underwear with your hair in curlers.

Emotional Photos

© photo by Positive Light Photography

- The joy and tears of your wedding day are the subjects of emotional photojournalistic photography.

- In addition to reminding you of your most emotional memories, a good photojournalist will show you moments at your wedding that you never had a chance to see.

- If you know that your brother is going to bust a move on the dance floor and that your maid of honor is going to weep during her speech, let your photographer know ahead of time.

146

bride. They'll take a low-key approach with their involvement, and know where you are throughout your day, although you may not notice them until you need them. By observing and anticipating they take photos at what famous photographer Henri Cartier-Bresson called "the decisive moment."

For the best coverage, choose a photographer who mixes classic photography, photojournalism, and commercial photography techniques. Look for a talented artist who fills his or her candid shots with emotion and makes posed shots look spontaneous.

A Thousand Words

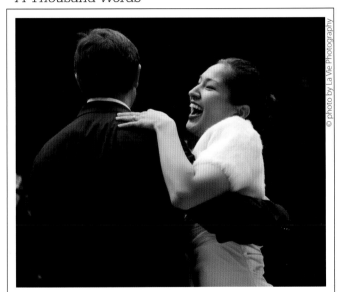

© photo by La Vie Photography

- The picture above of the bride dancing with her father discreetly captures the joy, trust, and love in their relationship.

- The best documentary shots happen when you don't know they're being taken. If you're not posing for a picture, keep your eye off the camera and enjoy your day.

- Once your reception begins, a photojournalist will melt into the background. Any posed shots you want throughout the night will need to be requested.

Stand-out Moments

© photo by GH Kim Photography

- Alert your photographer ahead of time if a special surprise like the one above will be part of your ceremony or reception.

- Passionate photojournalists don't let a little rain, or even a big lighting storm, get in the way of their photography. If you're into being out in it, they'll capture it.

- Life is full of the unexpected, and your wedding day is no different. With the right photographer, your unexpected moments will become images to treasure.

147

FASHION & DETAILS

Images that focus on fashion and details show off your unique wedding style

By combining fashion and commercial photography techniques, a great wedding photographer creates images that showcase your look and the details that compose your wedding style. You'll spend tons of time choosing your dress, your shoes, your jewelry, and your bridal party fashions, so why not have some photos that really highlight your choices?

Fashion-forward photos focus on the shape, texture, color, and details of garments and accessories—and the attitudes of the people wearing them. Makeup and hairstyles are highlighted, and backgrounds are carefully considered even when photos are not posed. Your photographer will probably require extra time before your ceremony to take fashion

Group Style

© photo by GH Kim Photography

- The photo above focuses on the style of the bridal party and looks like it came straight out of a fashion magazine.

- Rather than lining everyone up in a tight line that obscures the edges of dresses and suits, the

photographer arranged this bridal party in a way that highlights their attire.

- Notice how the background was carefully chosen to complement the style of the wedding and the color of the fashions worn.

Personal Style

© photo by Yours by John Photography

- Does being a fashion model sound like fun to you? Then go for it and strike a pose!

- For a flawless finish, have a trial run of your hair and makeup and consider having your teeth whitened.

- While fashion has become an integral part of today's artistic wedding photography, boudoir photography is now also on the rise. Many brides are having tasteful photos taken of themselves in luscious lingerie to give to their groom on their wedding night.

and bridal portraits, so be sure to add time to your schedule. If more time isn't possible, just remember to keep your shoulders back, your face relaxed, and your smile at the ready and you'll get lots of stylish photos that happen naturally.

To add the finishing touch, your photographer will focus on the important details that make your wedding unique. From your cake to your calla lilies, from your grandmother's charm bracelet to the vows you keep practicing again and again, a truly outstanding photographer will have your wedding covered from beginning to end.

Fashionable Details

© photo by Yours by John Photography

- Special jewelry and sentimental accessories like the ring and necklace above can be photographed on or off your body.

- Your photographer will use detail photos to add interest and style to your wedding album.

- If you're interested in having your wedding published in a magazine or on a Web site that features real weddings, like JunebugWeddings.com, details will play an important part in telling the story of your wedding day. Send in lots of photos with your submission.

Sentimental Details

© photo by GH Kim Photography

- Mail your invitation, programs, and other paper products to your photographer prior to your wedding so he or she can photograph them in advance of your day.

- Photos of invitations, Ketubahs, and vows make great opening page shots for your album.

- Be sure to let your photographer know about any items of significant sentimental value to you that might get overlooked: a family heirloom, a special gift from your groom, a personal memento. Ask him or her to capture them creatively.

PHOTOS & VIDEO

HIRING A PRO

Find the photographer, pricing, and package that are perfect for your wedding

With so much to cover on your wedding day, how do you find the one photographer you're looking for, the one with the style, personality, pricing, and packages that will exceed your expectations? Begin by searching the Internet and asking for recommendations from friends and family. Pick at least five photographers whose style you adore, then meet with each one to see how well you connect. Ask to see portfolios of several full weddings so you get an idea of how each photographer will capture your day and how he or she interprets each wedding differently. Ask lots of questions and be absolutely clear about what you're paying for: how much time, how many prints, and what extras are included in each

Choosing an Artist

© photo by Junebug Weddings

- Your photographer will probably spend more time with you on your wedding day than anyone else you hire. Be sure you enjoy being around this person and trust him or her to capture you the way you want to be seen.

- Having engagement photos taken is a great way to connect with your photographer, get comfortable in front of the camera, and get great shots of the two of you before you're married.

Contracts and Details

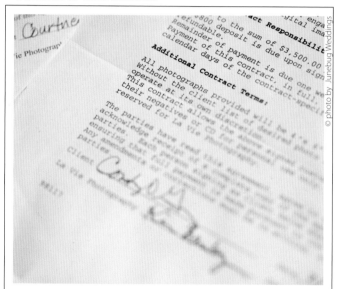

© photo by Junebug Weddings

- Make sure you get a signed copy of your contract from your photographer when you make your final decision.

- Ask what equipment your photographer works with, how much backup equipment will be carried, and what guarantee will be provided if he or she is unable to shoot your wedding due to an emergency.

- Extras, like albums, enlargements, and additional photos, can add up quickly. Ask your photographer to let you know how much an average client spends on these items after the wedding.

package, as well as whether he or she will be shooting digital, film, or a combination of both.

Digital versus film is a debate that has been going on since the late 1980s, and over the last twenty years technology has changed dramatically. Early on there was no question that film was of superior quality, but with the advent of new top-of-the-line cameras, lenses, and software, there is now little or no practical difference in the quality between digital and film. In addition, most digital photographers offer client galleries on their Web sites where your friends and family can view your photos and prints. And because digital photographers have the option to edit and print only the best shots through a process devoid of chemicals, it's a less wasteful and cleaner option for the environment.

Wedding photography has become a wildly popular career choice of late. No matter what style, process, or package you're looking for, you're bound to encounter a wide range of pricing and photographic quality that ranges from amateurish to truly artistic.

Digital

© photo by Junebug Weddings

- Digital photography allows photographers to take thousands of photos in a day and instantly see the results.

- To print beautiful quality digital prints and enlargements, you need high-resolution files. Find out if high-res files are included in your package or if you'll need to purchase them separately.

- As in film photography, the processing and printing of an image helps determine its quality. Good digital photographers are highly skilled in "digital darkroom" techniques.

Film

© photo by Junebug Weddings

- Many artistic wedding photographers own large- or medium-format cameras, like the one above, that produce large negatives. These are still the preferred choice for enlargements beyond 16x20.

- Safely store your film negatives in archival acid-free sleeves, out of direct sunlight, and in a cool place where the temperature and humidity are not likely to dramatically change.

- Some people just love the idea of film. It simply appeals to their nostalgic, romantic side.

ALBUMS & ENLARGEMENTS

Show off your favorite photos with beautiful, creative albums and frames that match your wedding style

With a seemingly endless array of options and prices at your fingertips, choosing your wedding album can be almost as challenging as choosing your photographer. Look for an album that will stand the test of time while showing off the style of your wedding day.

Classic, timeless wedding photos look right at home in traditional albums filled with matted pages and covered in leather or high-quality fabric. Couples and their families usually work with their photographer to choose the photos included in these heirloom-style albums. The couple's names and wedding date are often engraved on the front or back cover.

In recent years flush-mount or "magazine-style" albums

Traditional Album Styles

© photo by Junebug Weddings

- Today's albums tell the story of your wedding day, even if they're filled with classic photos.

- Whether your photos are film or digital, most photographers prefer to use a mixture of black-and-white and color photos to make your album more interesting.

- For most of the last century, classic albums had a vellum overlay on each page to protect photos from dust and scratches. Some people still prefer that design for its protection and formal look.

Flush-Mount Albums

© photo by Yours by John Photography

- Digital photographers are more likely than film photographers to offer flush-mount albums, but these albums are available for both mediums.

- Flush-mount albums can look simple and clean, or be full of collages and manipulated images. Think

carefully before ordering an album that will look dated later.

- Albums are priced by overall size, page count, and the quality of materials and craftsmanship. Bookbound albums range from several hundred to several thousand dollars.

have become popular with couples and photographers. Usually the photographer or an album-design company creates artistic page layouts that include single or multiple photos per page. The images are printed directly on the finished pages, creating a bound album that makes a perfect coffee-table book you can leave out for guests to enjoy.

Making your own album can be a fun way to create a one-of-a-kind heirloom and save money at the same time. If you're savvy with publishing software, you can lay out your own album and have it printed. Or, if you're good with your hands, you can create and bind an album with fabrics and notions found in framing and craft stores.

In addition to, or instead of, an album, many couples design creative displays of their wedding photo collections to romantically adorn their bedrooms or to add portraits to their wall of family photos to carry on a sentimental tradition.

When it comes time to make your enlargements, you will need the film negatives or high-resolution digital files. Be sure you understand if these items are included in your photography package.

Alternative Albums

- Parents and relatives love to have their own small albums to share. Consider ordering extra "parent albums" to honor their contributions to your wedding.

- An increasing number of online companies are making it easy for you to design your own album from prints or digital files. Look to our Resource Directory to find some outstanding options.

- Accordion displays, standing photo screens, decorative photo boxes, and multiple photo mats are just some of the options available at framing stores.

Enlargements

- Many photo labs offer choices of photo borders on enlargements. A white border lends a more vintage look.

- Displaying your wedding photos in your bedroom can be a sweet way to remind yourself daily of your love and commitment.

- Be sure to mark where you want your photos cropped when you order your enlargements; otherwise the lab may crop them in a way that doesn't work for you.

VIDEOGRAPHY

Video captures the moments and memories that make your wedding story special

Today's leading videographers capture your day as it unfolds, then edit the moments to create a moving story of the most important highlights and events. Unlike still photographers, they're able to capture the sights and the sounds of your wedding day and add music to create atmosphere and transitions. A skilled and talented videographer can create a truly artistic short film that will make you laugh, cry, and watch it again and again.

Classic-style videographers usually set up vignettes, interview guests, and include footage of your entire ceremony from the processional to the recessional. More photojournalistic videographers usually do not include posed shots. They edit for overall artistic impact and don't always present an

Hiring a Pro

© photo by La Vie Photography

- Narrow your search down to at least three videographers whose work you love.

- Ask the other professionals you've hired who they would recommend. Your photographer and wedding consultant should be particularly helpful in this regard.

- Don't rely on online examples to make your decision. Be sure you see at least three full wedding DVDs. Watch for quality throughout and smooth transitions, and eliminate anyone with inconsistent camera or audio work.

Classic

© photo by La Vie Photography

- Classic videographers often interview guests and family members. Some add montages of the bride's and groom's childhood photos to the final product as well.

- Ask that there be at least two cameras operating during your ceremony and reception to cover events coming and going.

- Be sure your videographer uses wireless microphones so all of your ceremony will be recorded.

- Expect to wait several months for your video to be edited and ready.

entirely linear chain of events. However, almost all videographers will present you with a DVD that is forty-five to ninety minutes in length, including easy-to-navigate menus that take you from one part of your day to the next.

Today's videographers may be shooting in high definition. This medium allows for a sharper, brighter result and offers a wide aspect ratio that allows you to see your video on your television the way you see a movie in a theater. Be aware, however, that you may need a Blu-ray burner to take full advantage of this technology.

Photojournalistic

© photo by J. Garner Photography

- A photojournalist will be with you as the day goes by. You may catch his or her eye occasionally, but for the most part he or she will be invisible.

- Try to forget that the camera is on you and the footage will show off your authentic personality.

- If you have favorite music you want included in your video, let your videographer know before your wedding. It may actually inspire him or her to create something that complements it perfectly.

High-Def to Super 8

© photo by La Vie Photography

- Some artistic videographers still work with Super 8 and 16mm film that they subsequently transfer to a digital format. This creates a timeless, film quality look.

- If your reception site is dimly lit, be sure your videographer has sufficient lighting to capture it.

- Videography has changed dramatically in the last few decades, with new technologies constantly arising. Ask your videographer to let you know what equipment he or she uses and when it was last updated.

PHOTOS & VIDEO

SEASONAL FLOWERS

Locally grown flowers and fresh botanicals add seasonal flair to your wedding day

Nothing announces spring like a field of tulips or sets off a fall day like maple trees shining in the sun. Make your wedding date special by showcasing the blossoms and botanicals that are near and dear to you and that highlight the bounty of the season.

Celebrate the birth of spring by choosing botanicals that are the essence of fresh and new. Use blossoms that are just beginning to open and berries that are still ripening in your bouquets. Display potted centerpieces of miniature daffodils, tulips, and irises. Create favors of bulbs or tree seedlings to be given away as gifts.

Show off summer's bright personality by choosing intensely saturated colors. Whether you choose just one shade or

Spring

© photo by Junebug Weddings

- Tulips, grape hyacinths, alliums, peonies, and checkerboard lilies make up the spring arrangement above.

- Tuberose, freesia, stephanotis, and hyacinth are all deliciously scented additions to your bouquet.

- Monochromatic pastel color palettes look naturally soft and feminine, and bright color combinations stand out in bouquets and centerpieces.

- Which flowers do you love and notice first every spring? Incorporate some of your favorites into your bouquet and centerpieces.

Summer

© photo by Positive Light Photography

- Bright and vibrant colors look gorgeous at outdoor weddings, while deeper hues look lovely indoors.

- If you live where temperatures soar, choose flowers that are heat resistant for your bouquets, boutonnieres, and corsages.

- Return flowers to water occasionally to keep them from wilting, and have a spray bottle on hand to keep blossoms moist.

- Hawaiian flowers, like orchids, ginger halcyon, and bird of paradise, stand up to summer's high temperatures.

mix and match, you'll love the way bold colors look in your arrangements and photographs.

Showcase your casual fall style by incorporating beautiful seedpods and grasses into your arrangements, or create a more formal, elegant autumn look with tightly constructed floral arrangements of deep orange or yellow roses.

In a cold winter climate zone, try incorporating berries still on the bush, shapely branches or evergreens into your floral design. For mild climates consider using lots of white in your color scheme, then adding candles and twinkling lights.

Fall

© photo by J. Garner Photography

Winter

© photo by J. Garner Photography

- Look for dark foliage to add autumn colors to your floral bouquet, as shown in the image above.

- Chocolate brown, deep red, and burnished gold are obvious choices for a fall wedding color palette. Make your color scheme unique by choosing just one of these colors and combining it with harvest peach, Tiffany blue, or a creamy shade of white.

- Late-summer flowers, like sunflowers, black-eyed Susans, delphinium, and gerbera daisies, still fit right in at autumn weddings.

- Gardenias smell as divine as they look in the classic white winter bouquet pictured above.

- Candlelight creates a riveting focal point for winter floral arrangements and beautifully symbolizes the season.

- Amaryllis, poinsettias, holly, and evergreens are the traditional botanicals for weddings with a Christmas theme.

- Wreaths on doors and those used as centerpieces make lovely take-home gifts for your guests.

FLOWERS

BOUQUETS

Choose the shape, blossoms, and details of your most important floral arrangement

Next to your wedding dress, your bouquet is perhaps the most iconic symbol of your bridal style, so think of your bouquet as a fashion accessory to help begin your planning. Just like the other fashionable items you wear, your bouquet should complement your height and shape, coordinate with your dress, fit in with your location decor, and accent your personal style.

Small and compact arrangements like posies and nosegays work wonderfully with petite women or sleek simple dresses. Larger round or cascading bouquets pair best with taller women or dresses with full skirts, ruffles, and special detailing. Discuss your dress shape with your florist to find the right balance for you.

Classic

- This classic round nosegay is made from roses, tulips, calla lilies, spray roses, ranunculus, gardenias, and sweet peas.

- Lily of the valley, stephanotis, orchids, tulips, and tuberoses also make beautiful classic bouquets.

- A solid-colored ribbon-wrapped handle gives your bouquet a clean, classic-looking base and a handle that's easy to hold.

- Incorporate trailing ribbons or a decorative fabric cuff framing the bottom of the bouquet for luxurious texture and interest.

Casual

- The loose shape of this hydrangea, Queen Anne's lace, and peony bouquet gives it a casual, fresh, and romantic feel.

- Poppies, peonies, ranunculus, lilac, sweet peas, freesia, and delphinium are also lovely in casual bouquets.

- If you or your fiancé have allergies or are sensitive to strong scents, be sure your bouquet won't be overly fragrant for either of you.

- Tuck your grandmother's embroidered handkerchief around the handle of your bouquet for a special "something old."

Your reception location, decor, and theme can also guide your choices. A single bloom or color of flower creates bouquets that are refined and elegant, just right for a classic wedding in a glittering ballroom. Creative combinations of colors and flower types make for more casual bouquets with a fresh-from-the-garden feel. Add special details like ribbon-wrapped stems, charms, or brooches to complete your bouquet design.

Be sure your flowers will be delivered in time for your wedding day photos, and if your bouquet stems are soaking in water to stay fresh, keep a towel handy to dry them off.

ZOOM

Hold your bouquet comfortably at waist level, just where your hands naturally fall in front of you. If you find you're holding your bouquet higher and higher as the day goes on, you're probably feeling a bit nervous. Take a deep breath and let your arms, shoulders, and nerves relax.

Alternative

© photo by One Thousand Words Photography

- Wheat and berries make the seasonal bouquet above ideal for a golden fall wedding.

- Other creative additions that make a big impact in floral arrangements are succulents, fruits, fern curls, herbs, feathers, and seashells.

- Paper and fabric flowers make alternative bouquets that will stay beautiful long after your wedding day.

- For an ultramodern and architectural bouquet, concentrate on the shape and construction of the design.

For the Bridesmaids

© photo by La Vie Photography

- Give your florist a swatch of your bridesmaids' dress fabric so he or she knows exactly what shades of flowers to choose or avoid, or how to nicely match the ribbon on the bouquet handles, as shown above.

- For a harmonious and perfectly matched look, choose a smaller version of your bridal bouquet for each bridesmaid.

- Make each bridesmaid's bouquet from a single blossom in your own to showcase the special qualities of each flower and each dearly cherished friend.

FLOWERS

BOUTONNIERES & CORSAGES

Honor your bridal party and important family members with fashionable floral accessories

Presenting your bridal party and family members with boutonnieres and corsages is a lovely way to make them feel respected and a fashionable way to tie your bridal look together.

The groom usually gives a boutonniere to the men in his bridal party, including his ring bearer, and one to his father and father-in-law. He may also choose to bestow the honor on grandfathers or special male friends in his life. Once commonly worn by gentlemen as a daily fashion accent, boutonnieres are now worn on only the most special occasions, when men want to stand out from the crowd. Usually a single flower or small cluster of flowers wrapped with floral tape, cord, or ribbon, a boutonniere can be designed to look

Classic Boutonnieres

© photo by La Vie Photography

- A single red rose is the most classic style of boutonniere for a black-tie wedding.

- A red rose literally means "I love you" in the Victorian language of flowers.

- The boutonniere is worn on the left side of the groom's lapel. Flowers are pinned on the jacket rather than pushed through the buttonhole.

- Some tailors add a thin cord underneath the buttonhole, eliminating the need for pins.

Casual Boutonnieres

© photo by John and Joseph Photography

- The chartreuse orchid above sets off the groom's tie and has its own special twist that makes it look fun and casual.

- If your florist isn't staying to pin on boutonnieres and corsages, designate someone to do it as guests arrive.

- Mini calla lilies offer beautiful choices for boutonnieres, while hypericum berries, coffee berries, and ferns make stylish alternatives.

- Lavender, stephanotis, and gardenias are fragrant choices for boutonnieres and corsages.

perfect with a classic tuxedo or a casual suit.

Corsages are usually presented to mothers and grand-mothers by the bride. They can also be single or multiflower arrangements, and they're usually pinned on the right-hand side of a woman's lapel. Wrist corsages are also quite popular because they do not require pinning, which can harm silky fabrics. They look lovely with sleeveless and short-sleeved fashions, while hair accessories that can be worn behind the ear look beautiful on any female guest.

ZOOM

The Internet is full of videos with step-by-step instructions for making your own boutonnieres and corsages. If you're looking for a DIY project that's easy and fun, look no further! Check out the Resources Directory for links to get you started.

Corsages

© photo by Junebug Weddings

- Traditionally corsages are pinned on the right-hand side, but wrist corsages are worn on the left.

- Remember that corsages and boutonnieres are meant to be worn all day. Choose heat-resistant flowers that can go hours without water.

- Keep your flowers in water and refrigerated until they are needed.

- Choose flowers that are part of your bouquet to create arrangements with a consistent theme, and keep arrangements small or compact so they're easy to wear.

DIY Options

© photo by La Vie Photography

- Knights used to be given a flower from their lady in lieu of a love note. Learn about the "language of flowers" and send your groom a message by fashioning his boutonniere yourself.

- For decades baby's breath was the most popular accent for boutonnieres;

use feathers, ferns, or berries for a more modern look.

- Make cute flower head-bands for your flower girls or a sweet floral collar for your dog. Design flower leis to present to your parents.

FLOWERS

CEREMONY STYLE

Decorate your ceremony site with romantic flower arrangements and creative floral accents

Decorating your wedding ceremony location provides a wonderful opportunity to create floral decor to highlight your style. Whether you cover your location in flowers from floor to ceiling or add tiny extra touches to an already spectacular venue, your floral decor can add romance, beauty, and theme to your ceremony.

If you're getting married in a church, the most common places for floral arrangements are at the altar and at the ends of the pews lining the aisle. Altar arrangements can be simple and subdued, gently dressing up your ceremony backdrop, or over-the-top structures like trees, columns, or chuppahs, exploding with stunning floral arrangements. Be sure to discuss your

Classic

© photo by Yours by John Photography

- A single large floral arrangement at the altar looks classic and dramatic, while several smaller arrangements nicely fill up a larger area.

- Consider how many wedding party members will be standing to your sides when choosing the layout for your arrangements. Try

  not to crowd yourselves so you feel comfortable in the moment.

- Ask your floral designer to visit your ceremony location if he or she has never been there before, or provide your florist with photos and measurements of the available space.

Casual

© photo by John and Joseph Photography

- Scatter flowers or flower petals on the ground as a beautiful way to create an aisle if one doesn't naturally exist in your outdoor location.

- In a casual garden ceremony, use tin pails or watering cans as creative

  holders for your floral arrangements.

- Work with the rustic details already present and accentuate their personality; fill an old wheelbarrow with blooms, wrap floral garland around fence posts, and hang floral wreaths from doors and gates.

plans with both your floral designer and your church wedding coordinator and put them in touch with each other so there is no miscommunication when your wedding day arrives.

In outdoor locations you may have more leeway to get creative with your floral ceremony style, but you may also need less decoration if it's already naturally lush. For a seamless look, choose flowers that complement the existing vegetation and landscape and tie in your wedding color palette by mixing in accents like ribbon, fabric, paper lanterns, or luminarias with your floral arrangements. Think of decorating areas like the altar, aisle, backs of chairs, trees surrounding the ceremony location, and entrance to the venue.

In an especially urban ceremony venue, you could choose to complement the clean look with strong modern shapes like tall, thin calla lilies in square vases, or you could go against the grain and soften things up with full blooming roses, peonies, and ranunculus in curving containers.

Whatever your style, be sure that your florist has enough time to set up before your ceremony begins and that he or she knows your venue's rules and regulations.

Alternative

© photo by John and Joseph Photography

- Candles create a glowing and romantic mood for your ceremony and are often less expensive than flowers. Be sure to check with your wedding venue to find out if you are allowed to have open flames on the premises.

- Use branches, reeds, or other delicate but large natural objects to create dramatic arrangements that will last and last.

- Have a smaller bouquet made just for the bouquet toss so your own can be preserved or given away as a gift.

Fun Extras

© photo by La Vie Photography

- Hand out paper cones full of flower petals or lavender that your guests can shower you with as you walk back up the aisle as husband and wife.

- Give your officiant a boutonniere, corsage, or necklace of flowers to honor him or her as a special part of your day.

- Be sure you have enough flower petals for your flower girl to scatter during the ceremony processional and to practice with in advance.

FLOWERS

RECEPTION STYLE
Stunning centerpieces and original floral details set your celebration apart

Continue your wedding style throughout your celebration by choosing floral reception decor that builds on the theme set at your ceremony and liven up the tone for the rest of the event.

The average wedding budget allots 8 to 10 percent of the total wedding cost for flowers, and this number can reach higher if you want more complex decor.

For larger events, consider choosing an event designer who can incorporate your floral design with your lighting, tabletops, and decor. For smaller weddings a florist whose work you love can probably supply everything you need, or can recommend additional rental companies to complete your event's look.

When meeting with your florist, explain your color palette,

Classic

- Classic centerpieces like the ones above, made with lilies and gardenias, fill the room with sweet fragrance and add to the romantic effect.

- Most rental companies have numerous options for centerpiece holders. Choose the same one for every table for a stream-lined look, or mix up the shapes and heights of the centerpieces to add depth and texture to the room.

- Use similar flower arrangements to decorate your guest book table, the restrooms, and other areas around your venue.

Casual

- Rich, bright, colorful blooms add cheer and excitement to your wedding reception. Be sure the existing decor at your venue will coordinate and not clash with your bold color choices.

- Sometimes centerpieces make it difficult for guests to see the people across the table from them. Keep them low and wide or tall and slim for easy socializing.

- Add a few small votive candles to your arrangements for some warmth and sparkle when the lights go down.

wedding party's attire, theme, and mood you want to create. Give the florist three adjectives to describe your ideal event, along with magazine and Web site images that inspire you.

Make the most of your floral decor by repurposing the arrangements from your ceremony. Vases on the head table, around the wedding cake, or on another surface needing attention will safely hold and showcase the wedding party bouquets. Use large arrangements and candles from around the altar to decorate a stage, buffet table, or entryway. Arrange for your florist or coordinator to be in charge of transportation.

•••••••••••••••••••• GREEN ● LIGHT ••••••••••••••••••••

After your wedding is over, what will happen to your flowers? All that beauty shouldn't go to waste, so arrange for them to be delivered to a local retirement home or hospital, or offer them to guests or vendors to take home at the end of the night.

Alternative

© photo by John and Joseph Photography

- Nonfloral decor that incorporates candles, branches, foliage, and moss makes dramatic and creative arrangements.

- Fresh-flower alternatives like paper and fabric flowers are a low-maintenance option.

- Use potted plants as centerpieces and send them home with guests as gifts at the end of the night.

- Instead of a traditional floral wreath, create one in the shape of your initials or monogram and hang it at the entrance of your venue to welcome guests.

Fun Extras

© photo by Junebug Weddings

- Hang garlands or other flowers from the backs of the guest chairs or just from the backs of the reception chairs for the bride and groom.

- Use fresh flowers to decorate your wedding cake, but be sure they are organically grown or free from harmful toxins. If you're concerned about this, use the fresh flowers on the cake table and sugar flowers on the cake itself.

- Edible crystallized flowers are beautiful additions to a wedding cake or any dessert.

FLOWERS

FUN & FASHIONABLE EXTRAS

Stylish floral accents add a finished look and flair to your wedding fashions

The possibilities for fun and fashionable floral extras at your wedding are truly endless and are limited only by your imagination. They can be used in everything from your table settings, guest book, and favors to your wedding party's attire accessories.

Individually potted sculptural succulents or fragrant herbs make welcome take-home favors and look charming as

tabletop decorations. For another lasting reminder, give guests packets of wildflower seeds or thank-you notes printed on handmade flower-seed paper that they can plant in their own gardens.

Potted orchids make beautiful and dramatic centerpieces at nearly any style of wedding, and they can be kept or given

Flower Girl

© photo by Positive Light Photography

- Instead of jewelry, give your flower girls floral accessories. A wreath of fresh flowers worn as a crown will make them look as pretty as a picture.

- For a perfect fit, measure your flower girls' heads and give the information to your florist.

- Rose petals, mixed wildflower petals, or whole small blossoms are wonderful for flower girls to scatter over the wedding aisle. Check with your venue to be sure they are allowed to do so.

Ring Bearer

© photo by John and Joseph Photography

- A ring bearer's pillow made from flowers is a superfun and creative alternative to the traditional. Be sure it's sturdy, and don't let little ring bearer or flower girl hands handle it too much before the ceremony begins.

- Give your ring bearer a boutonniere that matches, in smaller form, the groom and groomsmen's boutonnieres.

- Decorate your fabric ring pillow with fresh flowers that coordinate with the rest of your floral decor.

as special thank-you gifts after the night is over. The lush and densely grown green blades of wheatgrass look organic yet ultramodern in centerpieces and favors and can be a fun DIY project for a low-cost floral alternative.

On your tabletops tuck a single flower, fall leaf, or sprig of winterberries into the napkin at each place setting along with the evening's menu or the guest's place card. Pinecones, driftwood, twigs, and river rocks can also make simple yet elegant natural accents to help display place cards, favors, and information at each guest's seat.

Instead of using only flowers, consider fruit as a fun decor accessory. The soft orange color of apricots would look beautiful in a dish alongside pink, peach, and gold centerpieces. Pin a decorative seating card to a vibrant green Granny Smith apple for a gorgeous display at your black, white, and green wedding. Bright yellow lemons and green limes can fill the bottoms of the glass vases your floral arrangements are sitting in and add extra color to the room. Pile fresh blueberries, raspberries, and strawberries onto your wedding cake for a sumptuous summer design.

Bridesmaids

- A simple sash made from ribbon and flowers is a chic fashion accessory for any bridesmaid. Provide your florist with each bridesmaid's waist measurement well ahead of time.

- A fresh flower is a great accessory for bridesmaids. Every woman looks lovely

with a flower pinned to her dress or tied to her wrist regardless of her height, shape, or coloring.

- Instead of a bouquet, give each girlfriend a beautiful folded fan to carry with a single fresh flower at its base.

Accessories

- A pomander held by a ribbon is a lovely accessory for a bridesmaid, junior bridesmaid, or flower girl. Pomanders can also hang from the ceiling and playfully help decorate your event.

- As your guests arrive at your wedding, give each woman a flower to tuck behind her ear, pin to her dress, or wear as an accessory, and give each man a bloom to pin to his lapel.

- Carry a purse with a fresh flower pinned to its side.

FLOWERS

CAKE SHAPES & STYLES

Traditional shapes, delicate decorations, and romantic toppers make wedding cakes unique

Wedding cakes and breads have been a part of marriage celebrations as far back as Ancient Greece, representing happiness, fertility, and good fortune. Today's beautiful wedding cakes are a far cry from the simple breads used centuries ago and have become iconic symbols of the sweetness and romance of a modern marriage. They are not only delicious desserts but fabulous showpieces that highlight your personal wedding style.

Wedding cake designers range from commercial bakers to highly trained culinary artists and everything in between. Whichever type of service you choose, you'll want to meet with potential cake designers four to six months before your

Classic Round Shapes

© photo by One Thousand Words Photography

- An all-white wedding cake in a classic round shape is the most traditional option for a modern wedding.

- Layers can be stacked directly on top of each other with decorative frosting hiding the seams, or separated with pillars, columns, or other decorative supports for a taller and more regal effect.

- Wooden or plastic dowels must be inserted inside the cake to help support the layers and keep them from collapsing.

Classic Square Shapes

© photo by One Thousand Words Photography

- The cake in this photo uses delicate white-on-white frosting decoration to wonderful effect. The couple's monogram, the floral motif, and the smooth ribbons of frosting perfectly offset the strong square lines of the cake's shape.

- Square cake layers are a modern and dramatic alternative to the traditional round shape while still remaining elegant and refined.

- Square cake layers can be low and wide or narrow and tall—or a creative combination of the two.

wedding to see photos of their work and to taste samples of their cake flavors and fillings. The more complex the ingredients in your chosen cake, the more expensive it will be. Wedding cakes are usually priced per slice or serving, and cakes can be made to serve groups from fifty to five hundred, depending on your event. Additional decorations like elaborate piping, marzipan fruits, or crystallized-sugar flowers are dramatic and will be priced in addition to the basic cake. One way to keep things simple is to order a smaller wedding cake than you need and have a matching sheet cake discreetly sliced and served to additional guests.

Don't forget the extra cake accessories you may need, like a cake stand, cake topper, and knife and serving set. Your cake designer should have cake stands and service pieces available to rent, or you may want to find ones you love that you can save as keepsakes. If you choose to have a cake topper, get creative with it! Consider having one custom-made, or use a family heirloom topper for a sentimental vintage look.

Casual Shapes

© photo by La Vie Photography

- Fresh flowers piled high make even the most classic cakes look more organic and casual, no matter what the shape.

- Order extra flowers from your florist for your cake designer to use.

- The *croquembouche,* the traditional French wedding cake, is made of round cream-filled puff pastries piled high and decorated with spun sugar.

- Give a nod to your family by choosing a cake that's a regional specialty traditional to your heritage.

Alternative Shapes

© photo by John and Joseph Photography

- Unusual geometric shapes and unexpected proportions give this wedding cake an alternative twist.

- Consider three or four single-layer cakes arranged together, instead of one traditional tiered cake.

- Wedding cakes can be made in the shape of nearly anything you love, be it person, place, or thing. If you're interested in a truly unusual cake, designers who specialize in these works of art can sometimes ship them across the country, if necessary.

FLAVORS, FILLINGS & DECORATIONS

Creative choices of flavors, fillings, and decorations are the secret to a delicious dessert

Wedding cakes should be delicious to eat and divine to behold, and there's no need to sacrifice one for the other. With plenty of gorgeous cake designs and scrumptious flavors and fillings to choose from, it's easy to bring a sweet finale to your wedding meal.

Find inspiration for your cake flavors in the season, theme,

and overall style of your wedding. If you're throwing an elegant evening affair, delicate classic flavors like Madagascar vanilla cake with white chocolate and raspberry filling will match the atmosphere. If you're having a tropical wedding, look to exotic flavors like banana, passion fruit, guava, or mango. Choose light and airy citrus cake complete with lemon curd

Frosting

© photo by La Vie Photography

- Buttercream frosting, shown in the photo above, is rich and delicious, comes in many flavors, and is made with real butter, so it requires cool temperatures and careful handling.

- Fondant is made from powdered sugar and water and is rolled out to form a

smooth cake covering. It can be colored, cut, or sculpted to amazingly decorative effect, and it stands up well in most environments.

- Other tasty ingredients like cream cheese, chocolate, citrus, and spices can be added to frosting recipes to create specialty flavors.

Filling Flavors

© photo by Junebug Weddings

- Wedding cakes, like the citrus, berry, and white chocolate mousse cake above, can have multiple filling flavors between their layers.

- Classic fillings include chocolate ganache, buttercream, lemon curd, mousse, or vanilla cream.

- Liqueurs, like limoncello, amaretto, rum, Grand Marnier, and espresso, can be soaked into your cake.

- Bavarian cream and fresh fruit make wonderful seasonal cake fillings.

and mousse filling for an outdoor spring wedding, or a decadent mocha cake filled with chocolate ganache and toasted hazelnuts for a romantic winter celebration. If you and your partner have special cake flavors you adore, let your personalities shine through by choosing different flavors for each layer and letting your guests choose their favorite.

When it comes to cake decorations, let yourself be inspired by special wedding details like your flowers, your invitation design, your color palette, or the architecture of your wedding location. Practical considerations like the climate and length of your event should also be considered. Some types of frostings and decorative accents hold up to the heat and long hours better than others, and some may need refrigeration or special handling that your reception site manager should be made aware of well in advance.

Experienced wedding cake designers know the limitations of a cake's ingredients and structure and can guide you in the right direction while at the same time creating nearly anything your imagination can dream up. Meet with several different professionals to find the one who can best bring your vision to life.

Cake Flavors

© photo by La Vie Photography

- Chocolate is a perennially popular wedding cake flavor. Get creative with variations like red velvet, dark chocolate, or mocha.

- White cake is the most traditional cake flavor. It can be combined with almost any kind of filling and frosting.

- Carrot cake and spice cake have gained popularity at weddings, though their dense texture may make it difficult to stack the layers too high.

- Other common cake flavors are lemon poppy seed, almond, orange blossom, and banana.

Decorations

© photo by Junebug Weddings

- Have a matching stand custom-made like the one in the photo above, or find one that coordinates with your wedding theme.

- Flowers made from sugar paste or marzipan can be made to look like real-life flowers or can be whimsical interpretations of nature.

- Real flowers should be free from pesticides and chemicals.

- Seasonal fruits make beautiful decorations. Use berries in the spring and summer and pears, apples, or figs in the fall and winter.

CAKE ALTERNATIVES

Cupcakes, pies, and other desserts offer a delicious alternative to traditional wedding cake

If a classic tiered wedding cake doesn't ring your bell, then by all means serve your guests a mouthwatering sweet alternative that does.

Cupcakes have become a wildly popular wedding cake alternative, and for good reason. Who can resist them? They are small, adorable, and delicious, and you don't have to worry about

coordinating the cake cutting and serving. Each guest can simply take the cupcake they want to enjoy during your party.

If pies and tarts are your favorite desserts, why not serve them at your wedding? A table loaded with a selection of fresh berry, fruit, nut, or cream pies is sure to be a big hit. To sweeten the deal, have whipped cream, vanilla ice cream,

Cupcakes

© photo by Positive Light Photography

- Choose a selection of cupcake flavors and a single way to decorate them to keep your look cohesive.

- A tower of cupcakes on a multilayered cake stand looks impressive and echoes the traditional shape of a tiered wedding cake.

- When it comes time to cut the cake, a small cake set on top of your cupcake tower allows you to have the traditional cake cutting and a fun topper for your cupcake display.

Pies

© photo by Junebug Weddings

- Find pretty cake stands and platters to display your pies and tarts in a beautiful way.

- If you have numerous treats available, label the flavors of pies offered so guests know what their choices are and can avoid any they may have allergies to.

- Serve pies made from a family recipe and hand out pretty recipe cards as wedding favors. Include the story of where the recipe came from and why it's so special.

and candied nuts available to top each slice.

Minicakes make a big impact and each guest will feel honored to receive a special, personal confection. Serve them to each person at the end of a seated dinner, or create an impressive display of all the minicakes together so guests can choose their favorite.

To add a little whimsy to your event, ice-cream sundae bars, snow-cone machines, cotton candy, and dessert buffets are wonderful alternatives to wedding cake that will get your guests involved in the fun.

ZOOM

See the Resources Directory for businesses that supply individual ice-cream servings and old-fashioned ice-cream treats that are hard to find at most retail stores. Be sure to order enough to feed all your guests, plus a few extra in case some are damaged during shipping.

Minicakes

© photo by Junebug Weddings

- Minicakes are a fun way to serve wedding cake in a whole new way. Choose a design that plays up your wedding color scheme like the baby blue and white minicakes shown above.

- Serve minicakes that are miniature versions of a traditional tiered wedding cake. Cut and feed each other the mini version, just as you would a large cake.

- Minicakes make great take-home wedding favors so guests are left with a sweet treat from your celebration.

Unique Treats

© photo by Junebug Weddings

- Pass trays full of delectable little sweets during cocktail hour that are a preview of the dessert to come later in the evening.

- A dessert buffet full of petit fours, tartlets, cookies, brownies, and chocolates is delightful at the end of any wedding reception, whether it's in addition to a wedding cake or as an alternative.

- Old-fashioned frozen treats, like Popsicles, ice-cream sandwiches, and ice-cream cones, will make your guests feel like kids again.

FOOD & COCKTAILS

GROOM'S CAKE & NOVELTIES
Sweet treats, candies, and cakes for the groom are tasteful menu additions

If the two of you love desserts, there's always room on the menu for more. Fun additions of groom's cakes, candy buffets, and other treats can be a big hit!

Long ago slices of the groom's cake were sent home with single female guests. They were to put them under their pillows as they slept so they would dream of the man they were going to marry. These days groom's cakes are whimsical additions to any wedding and can be served as an alternative flavor to the wedding cake or boxed and taken home as favors for everyone. Many brides surprise their groom with a cake to fit his personality, while other couples have fun ordering these unique cakes together.

Groom's Cakes

© photo by La Vie Photography

- Perfect for a sports lover, the football cake shown above looks just like the real thing but tastes oh-so-much better!

- Have a groom's cake made in a shape that represents his favorite hobby, his profession, or his hometown.

- Groom's cakes are more popular in Southern weddings, but they're gaining popularity all over the country.

- Traditionally the groom's cake was a rich chocolate flavor and the wedding cake, also called the bride's cake, was a light white cake.

Chocolate

© photo by Positive Light Photography

- Chocolate-covered strawberries are classic and elegant wedding desserts. Pass them on trays, include them in a dessert buffet, or serve them alongside wedding cake slices for extra sweetness.

- Chocolate fondue is a warm, yummy dessert option.

- Rent a chocolate fountain from a local company, but be sure someone on-site knows how to maintain it so the chocolate doesn't run low or get clogged.

- Delectable chocolate truffles are perfect wedding favors that are sure to delight most every guest.

Candy buffets are as much decorations as they are yummy favors, so you'll want to have enough candy to create an abundant presentation. Choose five to ten varieties of candy and purchase several pounds of each depending on the size of your wedding and the look you're going for. Don't go under one-quarter to one-half a pound of candy per person, or you many run too low. Hard or wrapped candies work well in warmer climates, but the best choices are candies that you personally love and think your guests will appreciate.

Custom Cookies

© photo by Junebug Weddings

- Custom wedding cookies can be made in any shape, size, or personality. The darling cookies shown above represent the bridal party and would look great creatively displayed at a reception.

- Photo images can be printed on cookies in edible sugar ink. See our Resources Directory for companies that specialize in this art form.

- Serve your favorite cookies at your wedding reception, and then send guests home with a charming jar filled with extras or with dry mix, instructions, and the original recipe.

Candy Buffet

© photo by Yours by John Photography

- Include a small metal scoop in each candy jar for easy use.

- Small Chinese food–style takeout containers, vellum or clear plastic envelopes tied with ribbon, or pretty tins make excellent take-home containers for your candy buffet.

- Label each kind of candy, especially those containing nuts, so your guests can choose wisely in case of health concerns.

- A varying selection of large and small glass vases, bowls, and platters makes a charming candy buffet presentation.

FOOD & COCKTAILS

CATERING MENU
Treat your guests to a mouthwatering feast that fits your style and budget

When it comes to your wedding, food can be the largest cost of your event, and the difference in price between a classic plated dinner and an hors d'oeuvres reception is quite large. Look at all of your options creatively, interview different caterers, and consider your budget in order to choose the best option for you.

A seated dinner, which is the most formal choice, can consist of simply an appetizer, entree, and dessert, or be a more elaborate meal with five full courses or more, including palate cleansers and wine pairings. Buffets tend to lend a more casual feel and allow you to offer your guests more food options on a more flexible schedule. Alternative menus like picnics,

Classic

© photo by GH Kim Photography

- A plated dinner allows your guests to relax and have more time to visit with other people at their table.

- You can serve a single entree to everyone or offer guests entree options. This can be organized in advance through your wedding invitations, or guests can order from their server at the reception itself.

- Even if you don't offer guests choices for their main course, be sure to have some vegetarian options on hand for your non-meat-eating guests.

Casual

© photo by Positive Light Photography

- Be sure your buffet has space on either side to walk easily, and plenty of serving platters so guests can move through quickly.

- Smaller buffet stations can be spread throughout the reception hall to encourage mingling and create an interactive food experience.

- Specialty buffets that have a themed focus can support your larger wedding vision. Choose a regional focus like Italian, French, or Japanese foods, or highlight the local specialties from your own area.

culturally themed meals, or dessert-only receptions add fun to an event and incorporate your personal wedding style.

When hiring a caterer, you'll want to look over your contract carefully and be very specific with what you are asking for. A typical contract should include the complete menu, the number of guests and courses, tableware rental if provided, the date your final guest count is due, the number of servers and kitchen staff the caterer guarantees, gratuity, tax, deposit, and payment requirements, as well as policies about leftovers, overtime, cancellations, and liability.

Alternative

© photo by GH Kim Photography

- A reception of heavy hors d'oeuvres can be a lower-cost alternative to a sit-down dinner or buffet and still offer guests a delicious light meal. Be sure to specify this kind of food service on your invitation.

- Draw food inspiration from the seasons. Have

a summer barbecue, a spring garden picnic, a fall harvest-themed feast, or a winter champagne dessert reception.

- Morning weddings and elegant brunch receptions allow for creative breakfast-inspired menus and cocktails.

Playful Additions

© photo by La Vie Photography

- Late-night events need extra nourishment to fuel the dance party; miniburgers and fries are always a hit.

- Send guests home with tasty midnight snacks like donuts and chocolate milk, or give them a delicious morning after with locally

made pastries, homemade granola, and specialty coffees and teas.

- At a small, intimate hors d'oeuvres reception, make great food a main focus. Have an open kitchen area so guests can watch the chef and skilled kitchen staff in action.

FOOD & COCKTAILS

COCKTAILS & BEVERAGES
Innovative drink recipes add a refreshing touch to your reception menu

Celebrating with delicious drinks and toasting to your marriage goes hand in hand with wedding tradition, but the bar tab at your wedding can easily become the second-largest cost next to the food. Having an open bar with unlimited drink options is wonderful if your budget allows for it, but if not, don't fear; there are many other options available.

A cash bar, where guests buy their own drinks, could reduce your costs but is generally considered an etiquette faux pas. Your best bet for saving money is to cut down on the alcoholic drinks available and offer guests a simple selection of beer, wine, and soft drinks. If you love the idea of cocktails, choose a specialty drink designed just for the occasion or a

Champagne, Beer, and Wine

© photo by GH Kim Photography

- If wine is a passion of yours, play up its presence and showcase the special options your guests can choose from. If not, simply having one good white and one good red is perfectly acceptable.

- Delicious sparkling wines from the United States

and Prosecco from Italy make perfect alternatives to expensive French champagnes.

- Microbreweries are popping up all over the country, so great handcrafted beer is everywhere. Choose a local beer or two for your guests to enjoy.

Custom Cocktails

© photo by La Vie Photography

- Ask your caterer to create a custom cocktail for each of you, and let guests choose which flavor they enjoy best.

- Serve a signature cocktail from your favorite restaurant, the place where you got engaged, or your upcoming honeymoon location.

- To save time and cut down the bar line, your bartender may want to mix up some ingredients in advance.

- Name your custom cocktail creatively, then leave a menu card at the bar highlighting its ingredients and story.

limited number of liquors and mixers so you won't be surprised by the bar tab at the end of the night.

Depending on your event venue and the state you live in, there may be extra considerations regarding liquor licenses. Many locations already own one, but those that don't host a lot of events may not. Ask your venue about this early in the process so you have ample time to apply for the proper permits or come up with creative alternatives.

ZOOM

When it comes time for the toasts, be sure there is a nonalcoholic option like sparkling cider easily accessible for kids and guests who don't drink. Your waitstaff can give guests the option if they're passing out glasses, or guests can choose either from the bar.

Nonalcoholic Drinks

© photo by Positive Light Photography

- Set up an attractive, self-serve area for water and nonalcoholic drinks so guests can help themselves instead of waiting in line for the bar.

- Lemonade is a classic nonalcoholic drink and can be infused with strawberry, mint, or lavender.

- Label alcoholic and non-alcoholic drinks carefully so guests and parents will know which drinks to choose.

- Fun drinks for kids like Shirley Temples, root beer floats, and Italian sodas will make them feel special, like the adults.

Beverage Extras

© photo by Barbie Hull Photography

- Specialty glassware will make the drinks at your reception feel more elegant. Be sure you have enough appropriate glasses for champagne, wine, beer, cocktails, and nonalcoholic drinks.

- Soda and wine bottles can be custom ordered with labels that feature your wedding date, wedding logo, or a photo of the two of you; these make great wedding favors.

- A special set of champagne flutes for the two of you can make your toasts even more special and become lovely family heirlooms.

FOOD & COCKTAILS

179

CEREMONY MUSIC

From lilting solos to regal arrangements, music sets the tone for your ceremony

To find ceremony music that you'll love from your walk down the aisle to your exit, look for songs that fit your location and create the emotion you're looking for.

If you're getting married in a church or synagogue, you will need to consult with your officiant and the music director. You may discover there are restrictions on your selections and that recorded music is not allowed. Musicians may be provided or you may have to hire musicians to perform your choices. Don't worry! Chances are you still have many lovely options to choose.

If you're getting married at another location or by a nondenominational minister, you'll most likely have an open field

Classic

- Your church may have an accomplished organist, pianist, or even a gospel choir you can hire.

- Songs performed on the harp are perfect for classic, fairy-tale weddings.

- Pieces from Mendelssohn, Handel, Mozart, Bach, and

Pachelbel are classic ceremony choices that can be played by a live music duo, trio, or quartet.

- Some churches will allow secular music during your ceremony. Check with the clergy if you would like more flexibility in your musical choices.

Casual

- Acoustic guitar, fiddle, and mandolin are all lovely instruments for country casual weddings.

- Be sure that your music is loud enough to be heard well in your location.

- Choose songs from your first date together, your

most memorable trip, or your favorite band, or pick cultural songs that honor your family backgrounds.

- Have a favorite song with some words that don't quite fit? Rewrite them and create your own version.

when it comes to your choice of music and whether it's live or taped.

Regardless, you'll want to choose music for your prelude, processional, interlude, recessional, and postlude. The prelude should begin thirty minutes before your ceremony and set the tone for the rest of your ceremony. Your processional (or big walk down the aisle) should be a dramatic tune played at a tempo you can gracefully walk to. This song is meant to convey openhearted anticipation, and it can be quiet and reflective or joyous and exciting, depending on what best fits your style.

The interlude takes place during your ceremony, so look for songs that symbolize your love and/or faith. If you have a friend or family member who's musically talented, this is a great time to get him or her involved.

Once you're married, your recessional will be all about joyously celebrating your new life together. Whether your tastes lean more toward Beethoven or Bon Jovi, have fun choosing music that's unique, triumphant, and uplifting for this part of your day, and follow it with postlude music that plays until your last guest has made an exit.

Alternative

© photo by GH Kim Photography

- Gospel choirs or other music ensembles are dynamic additions to any wedding.

- Choose Latin jazz, Caribbean steel drums, or a voodoo lounge–style band. They make great alternatives to classic ensembles,

and you'll have a blast dancing your way out at the end of your ceremony.

- Choose a fun theme and create a score you love that's all from the Beatles, the 1920s, or the latest indie rock.

Considerations

© photo by J. Garner Photography

- Choose your ceremony musicians early; sought-after musicians are often booked up a year in advance.

- Pay special attention to the acoustics of your site and choose music that will fill the space without overpowering it.

- If you're getting married outdoors, be sure there is available electricity and adequate coverage in case of rain.

- For help finding the right music, ask your vocalist, bandleader, or wedding consultant for advice.

DANCE LESSONS
Learning the right moves gives you confidence from your first dance to your last

Your much-anticipated first dance will kick off the party part of your reception and set the tone for the entertainment to follow. Whether you're an avid dancer or a somewhat more reluctant participant, you can ensure that your time in the spotlight feels comfortable and looks fabulous to your guests by choosing the right moves and music.

To get started, choose your first-dance song at least three to six months before your wedding date. Pick five tunes each that fit the style of your reception, then choose the one you both love the most. While old standards are popular at formal events and pop tunes are frequently heard at semiformal affairs, your choice of music can be as unique as you are.

Classic First Dances

© photo by Yours by John Photography

- Follow in the footsteps of thousands of lucky couples before you by choosing a classic song like "As Time Goes By" from *Casablanca*, "Unforgettable" by Nat King Cole, or "The Best Is Yet to Come" from Frank Sinatra.

- Waltz or tango your way across the room to bring a formal touch to your first dance.

- Finish your dance with a big dip to end on a classic note.

- Ballroom dancing lessons are available in most cities. Do a local search for options near you.

Casual First Dances

© photo by La Vie Photography

- New classics are evolving all the time from the latest new music releases. Choose something from your favorite new band.

- Want to put a smile on your guests' faces and even make them giggle? Try dancing to James Brown's "I Feel Good" or Frank Sinatra's "Ain't That a Kick in the Head," or choose a song from your favorite romantic movie and ham it up.

- Learn to salsa, line dance, or tap dance to add an alternative touch to your reception.

Think outside the box and have fun finding a song that really resonates with the two of you.

Once you've decided on "your song," you'll want to practice dancing to it several times, or consider taking dance lessons to help you wow your guests and put your nerves at ease. Many couples today are taking their first dance to a whole new level by learning to tango, fox-trot, or break dance. What a fabulously romantic date idea and a great way to bring fun to your future!

If you're beginning your reception with an ethnic dance like the Jewish hora, the Greek Kalamatiano, or the Italian Tarantella, designate members of your bridal party to help guests learn the steps quickly, or have your DJ give a short description then call out the first few moves so everyone feels included.

Parent Dances

© photo by Jenny Jimenez Photography

- Include your parents in the song immediately following your first dance. Begin by dancing with your father and having your groom dance with his mom. Then dance with your groom's father and have your mom dance with your groom. Add grandparents, brothers, and sisters according to their ages.

- Choose a sentimental tune that everyone can dance to, like "Turn Around" by Harry Belafonte or "What a Wonderful World" by Louis Armstrong, and keep your handkerchief handy.

Cultural Dances

© photo by J. Garner Photography

- Few dances kick off a reception with as much joy as the classic Jewish hora, where couples and parents are lifted in chairs above the heads of circling guests.

- When you choose an ethnic dance, you honor your parents and grandparents and let guests in on what makes your background special.

- Cultural dances can represent regions as well as nationalities. Choose a line dance or Texas two-step if you're from the American Southwest or the Hustle if you're from NYC.

LIGHTING & DANCE FLOORS

Focus the spotlight on your style with creative lighting and dance floor options

To get your guests up on their feet and having a great time, you'll need to have a safe and appropriate-size dance floor that's dramatically lit for maximum appeal.

If your venue already has a dance floor, you'll want to make sure that it's level and has plenty of room for all your guests. If you'll need to provide your own dance floor, look to local companies that specialize in dance floor rentals and setup. Plan for one out of every three people to join in, and allot each person four square feet of space. You'll need to have subflooring, too, unless your space is completely flat, dry, and firm.

Once you've found a dance floor that works for you, look for lighting that can transform it from just fine to simply

Dance Floors

© photo by La Vie Photography

- Portable dance floors and subflooring are available through specialty rental companies in almost all urban areas. Most come in panels that range from one-foot to four-foot squares.

- Solid and checkerboard laminates and wood parquet floors are the most readily available options.

- If you're having an average-size reception of 150 guests, you'll need a two-hundred-square-foot dance floor.

Lighting Accents

© photo by La Vie Photography

- If you're planning to use candles, check with your location to be sure they're allowed.

- Candles placed against or on top of mirrors add subtle romantic light and make large rooms appear smaller.

- Choose colors that complement skin tones, like magenta and gold. Stay away from green, which can make you and your guests look pasty.

- Disco balls and track lighting create a club atmosphere, while chandeliers and candelabras create a chic ballroom effect.

184

fabulous. String paper lanterns or twinkling lights across the ceiling to create DIY accents that really make a difference, or go all out with a professional lighting company that creates dramatic lighting to show off your decor and transform your dance floor. Whether your lighting is subtle or dramatic, be sure your dance floor is well lit for your first dance, when all eyes and cameras will be on the two of you.

· · · · · · · · · · · · · · · *RED ● LIGHT* · · · · · · · · · · · · · ·

Lighting is one of the most overlooked elements of wedding planning when it comes to creating ambiance as well as safety. Be sure to light outdoor pathways and entrances, and if lighting comes with your reception site, give it a test-run to be sure it's up to your standards.

Commercial Lighting

© photo by John and Joseph Photography

- There are four types of commercial lighting techniques commonly used in reception lighting: pin spots, color wash, gobos, and LEDs.

- Pin spots are used as highlights to directly focus light on a small area, while color wash lights blanket large areas with colored light.

- Gobos, used above, are stencils made of steel or glass that are placed over lights to project a pattern or design that can be simple or elaborate.

- LEDs, or light-emitting diodes, use less electricity and create less heat.

Outdoor Reception Lighting

© photo by La Vie Photography

- Luminarias and strings of wireless LED lights project just enough light to safely steer guests on their way.

- Your photographer may be able to use nighttime lighting to create romantic slow exposure images.

- Tiki torches are the classic accents for beach weddings of all kinds. Add a twist by purchasing colored oil to match your color palette.

- Solar lanterns are available in a wide range of styles and make great green gifts for guests to take home.

WEDDING DJS

Begin and end your wedding on the right note with the help of a professional DJ

If you're planning on having recorded music played at your reception, then choosing a DJ will be one of the most important planning decisions you make. While you may have heard some horror stories of DJs who are too obtrusive or too corny, there are many more stories about great DJs who have made the night for brides, grooms, and their guests. So don't despair and don't forego hiring a professional to bring your event to life.

To find an experienced DJ whose personality and playlist complement your own, begin by doing a local Internet search and asking friends and coworkers for recommendations. Experience is crucial, as most seasoned DJs have learned to

Classic

© photo by Barbie Hull Photography

- Today's classic wedding DJs provide an eclectic range of music for crowds of all ages and are experts at transitioning from one event to the next.

- Your DJ should have high-quality audio equipment as well as backup equipment in case something fails.

- A classic DJ will wear a suit and tie or tuxedo to your wedding. If black-tie attire is important to you, be sure to specify that on your contract.

Casual/Alternative

© photo by John and Joseph Photography

- Many casual DJs focus on getting your guests to their feet and keeping them there with the latest dance tunes and club lighting that furthers the party atmosphere.

- Dance DJs beat mix music to seamlessly move from one song to another and build momentum throughout the evening.

- If you're looking for something hip and new, visit your favorite local clubs and see if a DJ there can spin for you. Be sure the DJ is willing to modify his or her behavior for your reception if necessary.

reflexively read a crowd and make the necessary changes in tone and tempo to keep your night unfolding as planned, so choose someone who has at least fifty weddings under his or her belt. Ask for at least five references from couples that have worked with the DJ in the last twelve months, and contact them all for feedback. Check with your other vendors to see whom they would recommend as well.

Once you've found a few DJs you're interested in, meet with them to find the one whose personality and playlist fits your style. Bring a list of songs that you would love to hear and those you would rather not. The latter is important because it lets your DJ know more about your style and ensures you won't find yourself doing the hokey-pokey or dancing the Macarena (just in case the idea gives you pause).

Make your final choice, then meet again two months before your wedding to go over the ages and musical tastes of your guests and create a final playlist that you all can be truly excited about.

Considerations

© photo by Junebug Weddings

- An experienced DJ should have almost all of your selections on hand. A short playlist is a sign of inexperience.

- Expect to pay a deposit of up to 50 percent to secure your date. Ask for a signed contract that outlines the company's policy regarding overtime and substitutions.

- Read the fine print on your contract and insist on meeting the DJ who will be present at your reception. Some large companies have been known to surprise couples by substituting DJs without their consent.

The iPod Wedding

© photo by Jenny Jimenez Photography

- Think twice before replacing a DJ with an iPod unless you have a trusted, outgoing friend who can act as your MC and a professional sound system to play your music over.

- Ask your friends to help create a playlist for every part of your reception. Put plenty of extra music in each one, in case you need to change your tune.

- Double-check that you have all the necessary adapters to hook your iPod up to the PA system.

LIVE BANDS
Talented performers create the mood, from background music to rock-the-house beats

Treating your guests to a live music performance brings an extra special touch to your wedding reception. Whether you hire a single musician to play background music during your cocktail hour, or a twelve-piece band to keep everyone dancing late into the night, there's nothing like live music to make a party feel special.

Once you decide on the style of music you want for your big day, start asking around for referrals from friends, family, recently married couples, and wedding professionals you trust. As with most things, word of mouth and personal recommendations are the best bets for success. Skilled professional musicians have busy schedules and are in high demand, so

Classic

© photo by GH Kim Photography

- Traditional wedding bands are generally made up of five to ten members with larger bands ranging up to twenty members. Check with your venue to see if there are size, power, or noise restrictions for larger bands.

- A great bandleader will have the personality to act as MC and make announcements when needed to keep the party flowing smoothly.

- A great band will be willing to learn a song they don't know as long as sheet music is accessible.

Casual

© photo by Positive Light Photography

- Sometimes unusual combinations are great as casual bands. A cello and double bass can interpret rock in a whole new way.

- Just like with a DJ, you should supply your musicians with a do-not-play list.

- Be sure your band plays a mixture of fast and slow, current and classic songs, so parents and older guests who may not be into tearing up the dance floor will have their chance to join in and enjoy the music.

it's smart to try to book them at least six months in advance.

In many areas you may work with a talent agency that represents many different bands and musicians. Be sure to get audio- or videotapes of the exact musicians you're thinking of hiring and that their names are specified in the final contract.

Live music contracts should also list their fees, the day's schedule, overtime charges, cancellation policies, liability insurance, meals, transportation, any special attire you want them to wear, and how many breaks they'll need so you can plan for other music during those times.

Alternative

© photo by Yours by John Photography

- If there's a special cultural dance you want at your reception, ask if your band knows the tune or is willing to learn it; if not, arrange for recorded music to be played.

- Have a favorite local band? Find out if they ever play private events.

- Honor your heritage with the appropriate music: Hire a bluegrass band, a salsa band, a Middle Eastern ensemble, an Irish folk music group, or a traditional Scottish bagpiper to serenade your guests.

Considerations

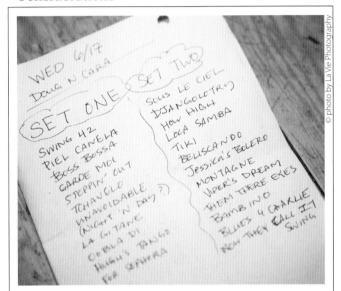

© photo by La Vie Photography

- Find out if you need to supply any equipment to your musicians, like chairs, music stands, lights, or speakers, and check with your venue to see if those items are available on-site.

- A full band may not be needed for the cocktail hour. Sometimes one or two musicians from the band can be booked to play together before the rest of their crew joins in.

- Personality plays a big part in performance; hire musicians whose personalities match what you're comfortable with.

FUN ENTERTAINMENT IDEAS

Surprise and delight your guests with unique performances and fun activities

Your wedding reception is the perfect time to get your guests involved in fun activities that fit in with the style of your celebration. From signing an interactive photo guest book, to watching dramatic performances, to learning a new dance, as long as you keep the pace of the party moving, your guests will be up for all kinds of fun.

Kids and adults alike love jumping into photo booths to get their pictures taken. These days there are options to rent the old-fashioned filmstrip photo booths or brand-new digital booths that show the photos on a screen for all to see. Many photographers can also work with you to set up a photo-booth area as part of your photography package.

Kids' Activity Area

© photo by La Vie Photography

- Depending on the ages of the kids, have a special performer you think they'll love, like a face painter, magician, storyteller, or caricature artist.

- Hire a babysitting service to watch over the kids' area so

parents can relax and enjoy the party knowing their kids are safe and having fun.

- Provide activities that the kids will love, like craft making, coloring contests, dress up, or sports games.

A Photo History

© photo by La Vie Photography

- Select the best photos of the two of you throughout the years and those that show the progression of your courtship for a photo slideshow.

- If you had recent engagement photos taken, include a few to represent the current versions of you.

- Set your slide show to music to add to the emotion and impact.

- Be careful to keep your presentation short and sweet; the energy of a party can suddenly fade if guests are forced to sit for too long.

Performances like photo slide shows, skits, songs, and professional dancers and singers bring an unexpected addition to the party and can keep guests entertained during the party's transition periods.

Kids can easily get bored at grown-up receptions, so create a supervised kids' activity area where they can let loose with friends their own age and parents can feel comfortable leaving their little ones to play. If there are special kids' meals for dinner, let them eat together so they won't get antsy sitting with the adults.

MAKE IT EASY

If you two are passionate about swing, salsa, or ballroom dancing, but many of your guests are not, hire a few professional dancers to attend the dance portion of your reception so they can give casual dance instruction, dance with your guests, and get everyone involved in the fun.

Performances

© photo by Positive Light Photography

- Traditional ethnic dancers and belly dancers can be exotic, energetic, and dynamic performers for a crowd of high-energy guests.

- If you love opera, hire a local professional to serenade your guests before the dancing begins.

- Dear friends who are professional performers themselves may be willing to sing a song or two during the reception. Give them the contact information of your DJ or bandleader so they can arrange what they need in advance.

Photo Booths

© photo by GH Kim Photography

- Old-fashioned photo booths are nostalgic and fun for everyone. Be sure there is a technician available during your event in case anything needs fixing.

- Ask guests to take some photos home and leave some behind so you both have mementos.

- Digital photo booths offer online photo sharing, which means everyone gets copies of all the fun photos.

- Include props like hats, sunglasses, and feather boas so guests can ham it up in front of the camera.

CLASSIC CEREMONIES

Time-honored traditions and religious faith provide the basis for a classic ceremony

Following family customs and choosing to have a religious authority to officiate provides the foundation for a traditional ceremony. Ministers, priests, rabbis, or other religious figures provide spiritual guidance to couples looking for a classic ceremony that's rich with time-honored rituals and blessings. No matter what your religious affiliation, choosing a traditional ceremony will most likely mean including the following elements:

A processional: Music will signal both mothers being seated and your bridal party proceeding to their set places near the altar. Your grand entrance and walk down the aisle will be the highlight, as all guests stand to see you in your dress.

Here Comes the Bride

© photo by La Vie Photography

- The bride may walk down the aisle with either her father, both of her parents, or alone, according to her traditions.

- The order of the processional will be prescribed by custom and varies between religions.

- Over 90 percent of brides still wear a shade of white.

- While most traditional ceremonies take place in a house of worship, more and more classic ceremonies are taking place at alternative locations, as an increasing number of religious officiants allow it.

Affirmations and Vows

© photo by La Vie Photography

- Time your ceremony from your guests' point of view. Fifteen minutes is too short, and two hours is probably too long.

- If you would like to customize your vows, be sure to check with your officiant before writing them. You may need permission.

- If you're having a religious ceremony, keep in mind that even if you've been attending services at the same place since childhood, you may not be aware of rules governing getting married there.

Opening remarks: Your ceremony will start with a welcoming blessing from your officiant.

Affirmation of intentions: For this important part of your rite, you'll proclaim that you've come freely to be married without legal impediment.

Charge to the couple and betrothal: Your officiant will remind you and your guests of the serious and sacred nature of your commitment, then ask if you promise to love and honor each other as long as you both live. Here's your big chance to say those special words, "I do."

Vow exchange: To affirm your intentions, you'll exchange or repeat vows. Many classic ceremonies begin, "I ____, take you, ____, to be my lawfully wedded husband . . ."

The ring exchange: As a symbol of your love and commitment, you will exchange wedding rings.

A pronouncement, followed by your kiss: To seal the deal, your officiant will pronounce you legally married and you'll be given permission to kiss. Stop and savor this moment! Then head back down the aisle to sign your license and celebrate.

The Ring Exchange

© photo by GH Kim Photography

- Your best man or ring bearer will present the rings to be blessed before you exchange them.

- You'll then present your beloved the ring as a symbol of your endless love, just as couples have done the world over for more than two thousand years.

- To be extra prepared, practice slipping the rings on at your rehearsal.

- In addition to elements highlighted here, your classic ceremony may be full of music, readings, and prayers.

Happily Ever After

© photo by Positive Light Photography

- "By the power vested in me by_____, I now pronounce you husband and wife; you may kiss" is the most common end to a traditional ceremony.

- After seeing you come in separately, your friends and family will watch you walk out for the first time as a married couple. Slow down and enjoy this romantic time together!

- Forming a second aisle of guests outside the church, synagogue, or mosque for you to rush down and make your getaway is a sweet, classic tradition.

PERSONALIZED CEREMONIES
Personal passions, values, and beliefs offer inspiration for unique classic and casual weddings

Whether your ceremony style is classic or casual, you may want to include some unique elements that make it feel more personal to the two of you. By adding a little or a lot of your own favorite music, poetry, rituals, and personal touches, you can create a one-of-a kind ceremony that's totally you!

Begin with the way your guests will be greeted. Will you have ushers? Then put a fun twist on it and have all the kids between the ages of eight and twelve you're related to do the job, or ask both sets of parents to greet people to create an intimate feeling. Planning on passing out programs? Then be sure yours are artfully designed to reflect your style

Down the Aisle

© photo by John and Joseph Photography

- Create a "sweet path" to the groom with your favorite fragrant flowers; they'll smell divine when they're crushed.

- Line the aisle with candles, garlands, or a hand-painted runner with your initials on it.

- Make your entrance in a gown of antique gray, rich cranberry, or pink champagne and cause a stir.

- Choose your brothers, a close male friend, or your pup to take you down the aisle.

Ceremony Events

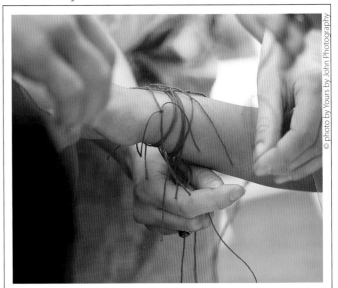

© photo by Yours by John Photography

- The couple pictured above literally "ties the knot" in a pagan handfasting ritual that inspired the saying.

- Look for ways to honor the coming together of your families. Have a sand ceremony, light a unity candle, or present your parents and grandparents with roses.

- When you write your own vows, you share a deeply personal side of yourself with your community and the one you love.

194

and consider adding poems, passages, or prayers that are important to you both.

Create a new twist in your processional. Have the groom walk his mother down the aisle before he takes his place at the altar, and just listen to the oohs and aahs from all your guests. When it comes time to walk down the aisle, pick music that plays to your deepest desires. Chose a trumpet processional to satisfy your royal princess fantasies, or have a bluegrass trio help you really "walk the line." If your wedding ceremony is nondenominational, consider creating your own vows and adding any special rituals that resonate with the two of you. If you're having a religious ceremony and you are unable to alter your vows, consider inviting family and friends to present poems, songs, and passages that are meaningful to your special commitment.

Once you've tied the knot, look for picture-perfect ways to make your exit, then head off to your reception in a Rolls Royce, a golf cart, a bicycle built for two, or whatever fits your style!

Involving Friends and Family

© photo by La Vie Photography

- If either of you have children, welcome them into your marriage by including them in your ceremony.

- Get your guests involved; have them greet one another or silently remember their wedding vows while you say yours.

- Make your own ring pillow with a special pocket. Use it as a tooth fairy pillow for your children.

- For a cute touch have all the kids in your wedding come down the aisle together in a wagon pulled by your best man.

Unique Recessionals

© photo by John and Joseph Photography

- Have your photographer line up guests on both sides of your exit. Give them flower petals to throw over you or pass out silver bells they can ring for good luck as you exit your house of worship.

- Bubbles provide a popular alternative to the ritual of throwing rice. Kids and adults love them, and they look great in pictures.

- Recessional music can be out of the box and perfectly tasteful. Make your exit to James Brown's "I Feel Good" or something similarly spirited.

195

CEREMONY ALTERNATIVES

Tie the knot in a ceremony that's as unique as your love for each other

Your wedding ceremony is all about making a lifetime commitment to the one you love in a way that is most authentic to the two of you. Fortunately there are lots of alternatives to choose from when it comes to creating a genuine ceremony that you'll both love and remember. Here are just a few.

Military weddings: If either or both of you are in the military,

you've earned the honor of getting married in full dress uniform by the chaplain of your branch and faith. Of course there will be rules to follow, so contact your chaplain to help you prepare as soon as you're engaged. You deserve exclusive treatment, and who doesn't love a man or woman in a uniform!

Military Weddings

© photo by Cheri Pearl Photography

- The Arch of Sabers pictured above is an honor reserved for those who have served or are serving in the armed forces.

- Commissioned officers and Marine NCOs are the only soldiers who can carry these special swords and sabers.

- A saber will also be used by the groom to cut the cake at the reception, and officers will be seated according to rank.

- Visit our Resources Directory to learn about military wedding resources and the rules and regulations that go along with them.

Civil Ceremonies

© photo by La Vie Photography

- The majority of civil ceremonies are held in an officiant's office at a city hall, but they can be held in any location.

- Judges, chaplains, mayors, county clerks, and justices of the peace are just some of the authorities who perform civil ceremonies.

- Friends and family members can be invited to witness your vows.

- Having a civil ceremony allows couples to get married on short notice and still have their marriage blessed at their church later on if they want to.

Civil ceremonies: Not just for couples looking for a quick, nonreligious courthouse ceremony, civil ceremonies provide flexibility and an inexpensive way to tie the knot where and when you want to. All you have to do is follow the most basic legal requirements, and the rest is up to you—plus you still have the option of throwing a lovely wedding reception following your ceremony or in the future.

Commitment ceremonies: If you're in love with someone of your same sex, you may be lucky enough to live someplace where you can get legally married. If not, you can still celebrate your relationship by planning a commitment ceremony. Other than some minor differences, beautifully planned commitment ceremonies are planned just like weddings.

Elopements: Want to get away from it all, or just be completely spontaneous? Then eloping might be perfect for you. Every year tens of thousands of couples take off to fun and dreamy destinations to get hitched without hassle. Just choose a spot that you adore and get ready to say "I do."

Commitment Ceremonies

© photo by La Vie Photography

- Opening remarks, vows, an exchange of rings, and a pronouncement that the couple is now joined are all included in commitment ceremonies.

- A reception usually follows, which can be as formal or casual as the couple chooses.

- A growing number of U.S. states and over twenty countries around the world, recognize gay marriage as legal.

- Turn to our Resources Directory to find links to gay-friendly religious organizations and reception sites.

Elopements

© photo by GH Kim Photography

- Over 150,000 couples get married in Las Vegas every year, because it's quick, easy, and legal. Be sure to check the requirements for your destination.

- Consider hiring a photographer to snap some sweet photos of you to send back to family and friends.

- If you're eloping to avoid sensitive family issues, consider how the news may affect those closest to you.

- After you elope, throw a party on your first or tenth anniversary to renew your vows.

CHOOSING AN OFFICIANT

Find someone you like, trust, and respect to officiate your wedding ceremony

Choosing a person to officiate your wedding is a very personal decision. You want someone who can represent your values and spiritual beliefs and speak from a place that truly represents your relationship.

If you decide to get married in your church, synagogue, or mosque your officiant will probably come with it or you may have more than one officiant to choose from. No matter where you're getting married, you'll need to reserve his or her time, make appointments for any necessary counseling, and pay a deposit to reserve the requested services (unless you're in the military, in which case your chaplain will perform the service for free).

Classic Officiants

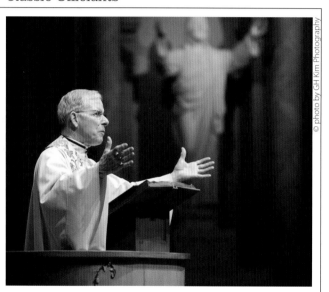

© photo by GH Kim Photography

- Getting married in a church comes with several requirements; talk with your officiant early to be sure you clearly understand them.

- Before you schedule anything else, ask how long the ceremony will take and how much time you'll have afterward.

- Some ministers, priests, and rabbis will travel to other locations to perform ceremonies. Ask, if this option appeals to you.

- Be sure your consultant speaks to the church coordinator to ensure the other's plans do not conflict.

Casual Officiants

© photo by La Vie Photography

- Many couples who believe in God or a higher power do not subscribe to all the rites and rituals of a particular religion. If this is true for you, choose a nondenominational officiant.

- Ask if there are videos available so you can see how he or she performs a ceremony.

- Conduct a local search on the Internet for wedding ministers and nondenominational celebrants. Look for Web sites with lots of client raves and a stated philosophy you agree with.

200

Many couples choose to have a nondenominational minister officiate their wedding in order to blend religions or personalize their ceremony. If that's the best choice for you, find someone with lots of experience whom you like and trust and who will listen to what's important to you. Ask for a copy of his or her sample ceremony, read it carefully, then ask any of the following questions that are relevant to you.

Can you personalize your ceremony? (Meaning, can you write or edit your own vows, include music and readings of your own choosing, or adjust the sequence of events to fit your style?) What restrictions are there on music, photography, or dress? Can you choose your own songs? Can your photographer use a flash? Will you or your guests be required to cover your arms or shoulders, or wear something to cover your head? What is the fee, when will you pay it, and will you be signing a contract? Does the officiant have backup in case of emergency? Can he or she attend your rehearsal and help with the processional and recessional as well as seating details? Then ask yourself if this is the person you want to have with you on your wedding day.

Alternative Officiants

© photo by Positive Light Photography

- Getting married by someone you know and love can be a heartwarming experience. Your sister, brother, family member, or friend can be "ordained" online to perform your ceremony.

- Online ordinations from the Universal Life Church are recognized in many states.

- There are celebrants who specialize in interfaith weddings, second weddings, pagan weddings, gay weddings, and marriages of every kind. There's definitely one that's right for you.

Details

© photo by La Vie Photography

- Be sure you know when and where you should sign the marriage license. It is the responsibility of your officiant to file this crucial document.

- If you are not familiar with the officiant you interview, ask for references and proof of their credentials before you give a deposit. Scams are very rare, but they do occur.

- Every state and country has different laws governing marriage. In Kansas and Colorado, for example, couples can get permission to perform their own ceremony!

WRITING YOUR OWN VOWS
Make a public declaration of your love by speaking from the heart

If you're looking forward to a classic, traditional ceremony, writing your own vows may feel out of the question. But if you're taking a more modern, casual approach to your ceremony, voicing your own feelings and interpreting your own commitment may be the only natural thing to do. If you're looking to personalize your ceremony by writing your own vows, ask yourself the following and write down the answers in detail.

Why and when did you know that your fiancé was "the one"? What memories do you hold most fondly of your time together? What qualities do you most revere in your partner? How does he or she complete you? What do you commit to do in order for the two of you to thrive and stay together for the rest of your lives?

Set aside time at least six weeks before your wedding

Write from the Heart

© photo by GH Kim Photography

- Write freely and from the heart without editing. Then go back and highlight what feels right for you.

- Consider your promises. Do you promise to love, honor, and cherish? How about being honest, forgiving,

or willing to seek counsel when times are tough?

- Have your officiant help you write your vows or look them over once you've written them. It can help to be sure you don't miss anything important.

Be Inspired

© photo by GH Kim Photography

- Let yourself be inspired by the first time you met or by a special time you spent on vacation, or plan a romantic weekend to spend together writing your vows.

- Weave in phrases from cherished books or music that you love.

- Use phrases that mirror one another. For instance both of you say, "I, ___, promise to support you through all of life's triumphs and challenges."

- Practice your vows several times before you get to the altar, and carry an extra copy with you "just in case."

to answer these questions with your partner and make a romantic night of it. Start by taking one hour alone to write on your own, then get together to share what you've both written. Check out the Web sites listed in the Resources Directory, which have lots of sample ceremonies to turn your thoughts into a ceremonial structure. Write a first draft of your vows, and then give yourselves a deadline for completing them (seriously, don't wait until the last minute and write your vows in a panic; you don't need that kind of stress). Once you have a good beginning, spend the rest of

the night celebrating how fabulous it is to be in love.

When you find yourself at the altar, remember there is only one person your words have been written for. Look into each other's eyes and forget about what anyone else is doing or thinking. This is a moment that belongs to the two of you.

Embrace Your Emotions

© photo by La Vie Photography

- Authentic words of love are guaranteed to bring tears to your eyes. Carry a tissue or hanky, or have your partner carry one for you.

- Use emotionally expressive words like "my beloved wife or husband" instead of "spouse."

- If you're facing one of life's challenges together, like an illness, military service, or raising children with special needs, consider making specific promises that address it in your vows. Marriages are about romance as well as real life.

For an Audience of One

© photo by La Vie Photography

- Holding hands during your ceremony helps keep you calm and present.

- Don't worry if you get choked up and have to pause. Your friends and family will be there to support you, and they'll feel touched by your emotion.

- Make a calligraphy copy of your vows to frame or add to your wedding album. Read them again on your anniversaries and throughout the years when you need a little encouragement to keep them.

203

SEATING

Smart seating arrangements get your party started and help put your guests at ease

Your guests will spend the majority of their time at your reception seated at a place of their choosing, or at one that you've selected for them. Their view of the events, the amount of space they have around them, and the company of the other guests at their table will all be factors in how much they enjoy the experience.

To create the most comfortable atmosphere, first consider the size of your venue and the type of meal you'll be serving. If tables and chairs aren't included at your location, visit a rental showroom to choose some, and bring a floor plan of your venue with you. Meet your consultant there or ask a salesperson to assist you. Once you've found options that

Seated Dinners

© photo by John and Joseph Photography

- The long table arrangement shown above is considered ultraformal. Many couples today use long tables in their design but omit the chairs on one side so the couple and bridal party can face the dining room without obstruction.

- Formal seating arrange-

ments frequently include individual seating cards that assign each guest to a particular chair.

- If you're renting tables and chairs without the help of a consultant, most rental companies will help you make a map that fits your needs.

Buffets

© photo by GH Kim Photography

- Round tables are most commonly used for events because they can comfortably seat the most guests per table.

- A sixty-inch round table fits eight people easily but not ten. Don't be tempted to squish folks together.

- Set out table assignments for your guests at the entrance to your reception. Then have your DJ or best man call your guests to the buffet one table at a time.

- Square tables are also available to bring a more restaurant-like look to the room.

suit your style and budget, use the map of your dining space and be sure that the arrangements leave plenty of room for people to move about freely. Choose chairs with padded seats or use tie-on pads to make guests more comfortable. If you're planning a cocktail hour in addition to or instead of a seated reception, use tall cocktail tables that make it easy for your guests to mingle, or go all out and create a one-of-a-kind lounge space complete with couches and pillows to help your guests relax.

YELLOW ● LIGHT

Creating a seating chart is a must and a social art that your consultant can't help you with. Before you assign your guests to seats, consider each person's personality and think of each table as a separate party. Combine people with similar interests who are likely to get along well.

Cocktail Tables

© photo by La Vie Photography

- Cocktail tables provide guests a place to put their plates and glasses while they move throughout the room.

- Generally used just during the cocktail hour, they can also be used for late-afternoon or after–dinner hour receptions.

- Some guests will prefer to be seated at a table, so keep that in mind when creating your layout.

- Shared tables can get messy quickly; use dark colors to hide stains, or lay an oversize napkin, which can be replaced, across the table.

Lounge-Style Seating

© photo by Raj Tents

- Decorative lounge-style atmospheres are all the rage of late. The space shown above was inspired by the luxury of Indian Mughal tenting.

- If you choose to create a cocktail atmosphere throughout your reception, consider leaving children off the guest list and hosting an adult-only party.

- In addition to party rental companies with generic tables and chairs, most cities have specialty rental and prop companies that carry unique furniture, lighting, and decor.

LINENS & CHAIR COVERS

Dress up your tables and chairs with stylish fabrics and fashionable accents

Whether your style is classic or casual, dressing up your tables and chairs with fabrics is one of the easiest ways to bring beauty and color to your reception venue. From rich velvets and brocades that shout "winter wedding," to sheer silks and organzas that show off a summer celebration, there is just about every weight, color, and texture available from specialty party rental companies.

Unless your tables are lovely to behold all by themselves, look for tablecloths that are floor length to hide any imperfections. Many venues offer shorter options that look too casual for formal affairs, so double-check before you go with their linen package.

Classic Linens

© photo by GH Kim Photography

- Ivory linens and chair covers look harmonious in the classic ballroom setting shown above and don't compete with the architecture, plus they were included in the hotel's package!

- If you're looking to dress up a less-ornate room, look for linens with bright colors or patterns that complement your color palette.

- Set up a mock table with a table setting to see how your linens, chairs, and tableware will look all together and in your venue.

Casual Linens

© photo by Junebug Weddings

- The "placemat" made of white rock and the starfish accent on the linen napkin shown above make a beautiful combination for a beach wedding. Look for accents that show off your theme.

- No matter how casual your wedding, linens will always look better than vinyl or paper.

- Don't forget to decorate your cake table. Cover it with a special cloth or sheer overlay. Put a draped screen behind it, or make it a focal point of the room.

Also, think creatively about your napkin choice; a specialty napkin and the right table accents can dress up a plain table-cloth and finish a look all on their own. Be sure the napkin fabric you choose is absorbent, and order plenty of extras to give to guests when needed and to dress up the cake and cocktail tables.

Once you've seen what your venue offers, visit a rental showroom that has table decor of all kinds. Take a photo of your venue with you, as well as any inspirational photos you've downloaded or torn out of magazines.

Decorative Chairs

© photo by La Vie Photography

- The chairs of the bride and groom are often decorated with special flowers, fabrics, or signs.

- Decorating your chairs can be a fun, inexpensive DIY project that helps put a finishing touch on your wedding style.

- Chair coverings range from simple tie-on seat pads that provide color and comfort to elaborately draped works of art.

- Simply tie a thick silk or velvet ribbon around your chair cover to add a splash of color from your palette.

Fun Extras

© photo by La Vie Photography

- A mini cornucopia of lavender and rosemary provides a scented accent to the plain white napkin above.

- Bring a fancy touch to your table by using an overlay cloth and "pickups" (small embellishments that you pin to your tablecloth to create a ruffled effect).

- Save money by adding accents to the options your venue provides instead of upgrading. Dress up your napkins with fresh flowers, ribbons, napkin rings, or elaborate folds.

SETTING THE TABLE

Tasteful plates, flatware, and glassware add a polished look to your wedding tables

Once the look and layout of your tables have been decided, move on to making them beautiful, functional, and easy to use by adding just the right mix of dishes, glassware, and flatware.

Meet with your caterer to determine the items you'll need for each course of your meal. Your caterer may be able to supply all the necessary items you're looking for, or you may choose to rent them. Discuss your dishes and glasses first. Set up a mock table with dinner plates, bread plates (if you need them), and glasses. Factor in the size of your centerpieces and leave extra room for condiments and your table card. If you're having a formal seated dinner, consider your utensils carefully. You may need room for an array of forks, knives, and

Classic Table Settings

© photo by GH Kim Photography

- A gold-rimmed charger is at the center of the classic setting shown above. A charger is a decorative plate that is not meant to hold food but acts as a frame for other dishes.

- The charger can be removed before the first course or at any time up until the dessert course.

- A single orchid adds beauty to the setting and sets off the black napkin shown above.

- If you need to create less clutter on the table, have servers bring new forks and wineglasses for each course.

Casual Table Settings

© photo by Junebug Weddings

- The table shown above is elegantly set for a country brunch reception in the spring, perfectly mixing both casual and classic elements.

- You don't need specialty china to set a lovely table. Use a colorful tablecloth, napkins, and flowers to dress up plain white or glass dishware.

- For a whimsical DIY approach, try setting every table in the room with a different china pattern. Borrow china sets from friends and family and create one-of-a-kind, low-cost table settings.

spoons at each place setting, or if you're having a buffet, you may not need standard utensils on your table at all.

Once you've determined what items you need, choose the options that best fit your style. White china with a gold or silver rim is the most popular and easy-to-find option for formal dinners, while plain white or glass china is most popular for more casual events. If you love the linens and centerpieces you've chosen, you may not want to add any more color or design detail to your table, and these options will work perfectly for your setting. However, if you're looking for something totally unique, try searching the Internet for specialty resources in your area to see what's available and ask your consultant or caterer for suggestions. When you're done setting your table, sit down and imagine you're a guest from start to finish. Putting yourself in their shoes will help you create a successful and unforgettable event.

Alternative Table Settings

© photo by Junebug Weddings

- The square metal chargers pictured above echo the shape of the table and give a modern look to the setting. Square dinnerware is available at most party rental companies.

- If you're serving a family-style meal, be sure that your serving dishes and glassware are sturdy so nothing gets tipped over when plates are passed.

- Do you collect candy bowls, salt and pepper shakers, or porcelain figurines? Add some of your collection to your settings for a unique, personal touch.

Fun Extras

© photo by La Vie Photography

- Table cards can be simply or elaborately designed with numbers or creative table names that match the theme of your wedding.

- Clusters of candles or cabaret lamps with pretty shades can help create an intimate nightclub atmosphere.

- Leave breadbaskets, candy dishes, bottles of wine, or specialty foods on the table for guests to share with one another. These additions will help break the ice and be appreciated between courses.

FUN RECEPTION EXTRAS

Delight your guests with thoughtful favors, services, and creative guest book ideas

Goodie bags, favors, creative guest books, and specialty foods and services are just some of the treats that make receptions extra special. If you're looking to go the extra mile for your guests, consider adding these optional items to your celebration. Here are just a few ideas to fit every budget and style.

Personalized favors: Crystal ornaments, silver bells, wine stoppers, CDs of your favorite music, and customized word magnets with your names, photos, and romantic adjectives included all fit nicely in little gift boxes and bring a smile to guests' faces.

Ecofriendly favors: Slip a pack of your favorite flower seeds on top of your guests' napkins, or create a centerpiece of

Personal Favors

© photo by John and Joseph Photography

- The tradition of giving out wedding favors dates back hundreds of years to a time when European aristocrats gave out precious boxes of metal, porcelain, or crystal called *bonbonnieres*. The boxes held five almonds or candies that represented love, life, success, happiness, and longevity.

- Many couples choose favors to match the theme, season, or location of their wedding or to highlight their cultural backgrounds, like rice candy or sake for their Japanese celebration or fiery hot sauce for their Mexican affair.

Organic and Edible Favors

Thank you for celebrating our special day with us!
Drive safely!
Love,
Jamie & Sean
September 2, 2007

© photo by John and Joseph Photography

- Who doesn't want cookies and milk for the ride home? Give your guests a peanut butter cookie and chocolate macaroon and you'll create a sweet memory.

- Family members can help make homemade favors, and it gives them a great way to contribute.

- Test ordered foods to be sure they're fresh and delicious before you choose them for your guests.

- Turn to the Resources Directory to find useful links to creative favor ideas.

potted topiary for your guests to take with them when they leave. Choose organic, locally made products and gifts.

Edible favors: Yum! Yum! Everyone loves homemade goodies like fudge and fruit jam. Make your own labels and give them out with your recipe for a personal touch. Don't have time to cook? Then choose a delicious treat that shows off the local flavor of your wedding location, like coffee and mugs for your Seattle wedding or chocolate macadamia nuts for your Hawaiian celebration.

Guest book ideas: The tradition of signing a guest book was on its way out of style until savvy brides came up with new twists like turning it into a wish book or having guests sign the mat of a large engagement photo instead. Think of your own way to make your guest book special, and it will be worth carrying on the tradition.

Specialty services: Depending on your location and specific needs, there is an array of services available for your guests' comfort. Hire a valet, coat-check services, a barista, or an artist to do caricatures of couples and their families. The options are as endless as your imagination!

Guest Book Ideas

© photo by GH Kim Photography

- Rent a photo booth or leave out a Polaroid for guests to take their own pictures. Then have them paste them into your guest book along with a special message.

- Display your matted engagement photo on an easel at the entrance to your reception. Get your family or bridal party to sign it first so guests will follow suit.

- Buy a porcelain serving platter that comes with a permanent marker for guests to sign. It will make a fun family heirloom.

Specialty Services

© photo by GH Kim Photography

- Specialty bars that serve espresso and other fun drinks are a hit with adults and children.

- Popcorn, snow-cone, and cotton-candy machines fit right in at casual summer weddings, while hot fudge sundaes and warm crepes are delicious in winter.

- Coat-check services help guests keep track of belongings and keep your gifts safe.

- Valets are truly appreciated when the weather is cold and rainy or when guests have to walk a distance from the parking lot.

THE BIG EVENTS

Sail through your reception's important events and enjoy being the center of attention

Wedding receptions are set apart from other celebrations by the romantic events and rituals that move them along from one touching moment to the next. To ensure that your event unfolds gracefully, arrive thirty minutes after the majority of your guests and have your best man or MC announce you. This presents a great opportunity to thank your guests for coming and welcome them to enjoy themselves.

Once you've made your grand entrance, give yourself another thirty to forty minutes to mingle with family and friends before the main course is served or the buffet line is opened. Traditionally you are served first, so take the time to get enough to eat right away and be prepared to move to

Toasts

© photo by Positive Light Photography

- Toasts should last one to five minutes and be focused on good wishes for both of you. Gracefully let speakers know your time limitations when you initially ask them to speak.

- Leave the open microphone for other occasions.

- Knowing who is going to speak and what they are likely to say can help you stay calm and collected.

- If you're having a video presentation, show it immediately before or after your toasts.

Cake Cutting

© photo by John and Joseph Photography

- When it comes time to cut the cake, put your hands on the knife together and slice off one piece from the bottom layer.

- Give each other one bite and then kiss. Do not smash the cake into each other's mouths; it's messy and not very romantic.

- It's customary to freeze the top layer to eat on your anniversary. If old cake isn't your favorite dessert, save the topper and put it on a fresh cake next year.

the toasts and cake cutting as soon as the last guests finish their meals.

Traditionally your best man, father, or friend will kick off the toasts and any presentations such as a video or slide show that you want to share with your guests. Be sure to organize this time well so there's enough time to include those who would like to speak and not so much time that your guests lose interest. If you would like to include more than six speakers, try scheduling their toasts between each menu course.

When it comes time to hit the dance floor for your first dance, go for it without hesitation. Your guests will be delighted whether you simply sway back and forth or put on a full-blown performance. Either way, you can't hope for a more supportive audience. To put the finishing touch on your event, you may chose to throw the bouquet and/or toss the garter to your single guests. If your guest list is light on people yearning to get married, choose another event as an alternative to these traditions.

Your First Dance

© photo by J. Garner Photography

- Dancing with confidence is no sweat when you've practiced or taken lessons. It's always a good idea to brush up on your moves.

- Some couples have their first dance when they first arrive at their reception. Do what feels best for you.

- Choose your father, his father, or your closest male friend or relative to dance with you next.

- Look into each other's eyes, smile, relax, and enjoy!

Garter and Bouquet Toss

© photo by GH Kim Photography

- The bouquet and garter toss originated back when a bride and groom had to give something away to avoid being mauled by their guests. Thank goodness today's guests are decidedly more civilized!

- To ensure a picture-perfect toss, try throwing a fake bouquet prior to your reception.

- For an alternative, design a "breakaway bouquet" with two parts to present to your mother and mother-in-law as gifts of appreciation, and save your garter as an heirloom.

HOSTING LIKE A PRO

Make it all look easy with professional tips for a flawless, stress-free reception

Creating a truly memorable wedding day isn't about how much money you spend or how many people you invite; it's about artful planning and accurately anticipating the needs of your guests.

Put yourself in your guests' shoes and consider the length of time you want them to attend, the distance you want them to travel, and what is likely to make them feel pampered while they're with you. It's easy to get overwhelmed by all the products and possibilities that exist for weddings, so taking a step back like this can help you make smart decisions.

Previsualize their experience all the way from receiving your invitation to watching you wave good-bye, and then plan how

Put Your Guests First

© photo by GH Kim Photography

- When people arrive, will they know where to go? Consider having your parents or members of your bridal party ready to greet them at the entrance of your reception.

- Imagine you're a guest receiving your invitation. Will they know how to dress, know who they can bring, and be offered a reasonable amount of time to plan and reply?

- Have you taken into account any special needs your guests may have? Will you need handicap ramps or child care for young children?

Create Smooth Transitions

© photo by John and Joseph Photography

- Light background music during the dinner hour allows guests to talk and get to know one another, while setting the stage for the dancing part of your celebration.

- To build momentum, schedule your dinner, the toasts, your cake cutting, and your first dance, in that order.

- If your venue has to be turned into a dining room after your ceremony, have a cocktail hour, scavenger hunt, dance presentation, or other entertainment planned in an adjoining area.

to keep them comfortably content from beginning to end. Carefully imagine your wedding day schedule unfolding to be sure that no one, including the two of you, is rushed from one thing to another, or left waiting around with nothing to do.

Consider what your guests will be seeing, and do your best to highlight the important things and make them forget about all the work behind the scenes. Plan your cake cutting against a complementary background, put spotlights on the dance floor for your first dance, and keep facilities, parking, and restrooms out of sight.

Don't forget that you're going to be the center of attention from morning until night, so plan your entrances and exits gracefully, with both you and your guests in mind. Have a place to relax quietly and gather your thoughts from when the guests begin to arrive until they see you come down the aisle. Arrive at your reception with finesse and allow guests to greet you. When it comes time to leave, make it a celebratory and special moment.

Think like a Photographer

© photo by John and Joseph Photography

- The classic, floral accented cake shown above stands out as a culinary work of art when paired with its surroundings.

- Think about where your guests will be saying their toasts and how those presentations will look from your guests' and photographer's points of view.

- Use candlelight, lamps, spotlights, and other forms of decorative lighting to create lovely ambiance and show off decor details.

Gracefully Enter and Exit

© photo by La Vie Photography

- Design your own exciting exit, like the fireworks send-off shown above.

- To end your day on a high note, post the end time for your reception on your schedule and leave before the majority of your guests do.

- Consider having snack bags for your guests to take home. Guests will welcome them after a long day.

- Far too many exits are wrecked by the overconsumption of alcohol. Have fun, but don't go overboard.

WEDDING SHOWER INSPIRATION

Bring on the fun and laughter with creative themes, gifts, and games

Wedding and bridal showers are fun-filled events that allow you to spend time with the people you love and start celebrating! Traditional bridal showers take place with the women in your life and are full of gifts to prepare your new home. These days there are no hard-and-fast rules for these events, and you may very likely have a number of them thrown in

your honor. The various groups could include both male and female family members, just girlfriends, coworkers, or other specific groups of people close to you.

Even though you aren't the one who is planning the party, do communicate your desires clearly and be gracious for all of the effort people put forth for you. Tell whoever is

Classic

© photo by Junebug Weddings

- Classic bridal showers include party games that involve the bride. Ask guests trivia questions about how the bride and groom met, their most romantic moments, and favorite things. Ask the groom ahead of time and then see if the bride can guess his answers.

- Luncheons can easily be hosted at home or at a restaurant.

- For lighter fare, schedule the event for the afternoon and have a tea party with finger sandwiches and hors d'oeuvres.

Casual

© photo by Barbie Hull Photography

- Invite the ladies over for brunch. Serve mimosas, Bloody Marys, French toast, quiche, fruit, and pastries, and send guests home with locally roasted coffee beans or homemade gourmet granola.

- Enjoy the sunshine with a picnic in the park. Bring

- lots of large picnic blankets, throw pillows, and some folding chairs for those who can't easily sit on the ground.

- Host a pajama party at home or at a hotel, complete with DIY beauty treatments and the bride's favorite snack foods.

planning the event (likely your maid of honor, your sister, or your mother) who is on your wedding guest list. You don't want to invite anyone to a shower if you're not also inviting them to the wedding.

Choosing a theme for the shower is a popular way to organize this kind of event. Since you may not need all the basics to start a home, a theme could be chosen that carries all the way through from the invitations, decorations, and food served to the games played and the kinds of gifts given.

You'll need to send out thank-you notes within two weeks of the shower, so purchase them ahead of time and get the address of each guest from the host of the party. As you open your gifts, be sure to have someone by your side to take careful notes on which gift came from which person. It will make writing thank-you notes infinitely easier, and you'll be reminded of the gift giver each time you use the item.

Alternative

© photo by GH Kim Photography

- Throw an evening cocktail party at a swanky bar or restaurant. Find out if the venue has a private area you can reserve, and have a specialty cocktail named after the bride.

- Get the groom in on the action and throw a coed wedding shower.

- For a beautiful East Indian–themed shower, serve yummy curries and flat breads and sweet mango lassis, decorate with jewel tones, and hire a henna artist to decorate each guest's hands or feet.

Thematic

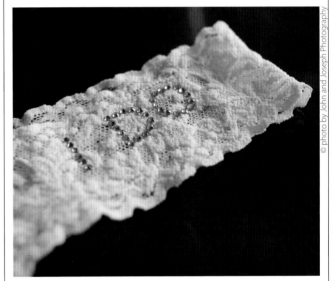

© photo by John and Joseph Photography

- A lingerie-themed shower will make opening gifts a lively event, and each item will be a welcome addition to her honeymoon wardrobe! Be sure the bride's sizes are included in the invitation.

- Let the bride's favorite hobbies lead the theme. If she loves cooking and baking, have a culinary-themed party with specialty foods and gifts for the kitchen.

- If she loves fashion, use fashion magazines as your decor inspiration and ask guests to bring fun accessories as gifts.

BACHELOR PARTY IDEAS

Say good-bye to the single life with a fun party that's just for the guys

The bachelor party is a time-honored tradition that shouldn't be missed by any groom. It's the time to kick back, relax, and celebrate your friendships as well as the big and exciting event to come.

Traditionally it's the best man's responsibility to plan the event, but he can always ask for help from the other groomsmen if he lives out of town or doesn't know all the guys involved. The best way to begin the planning process is for the best man to sit down with the groom and get a feel for the kind of party he's hoping for. Bachelor parties range in style from simple and subdued to wild and crazy, so a little direction from the man of honor is a safe bet.

Classic

© photo by J. Garner Photography

- Make a special toast to your friends. This is your chance to recognize their efforts in supporting your celebration and to say thanks.

- Take taxis, rent a car service, or stay in a hotel so no one has to worry about driving home.

- If you're going for a classic bachelor party, be sure your fiancée is comfortable with the plan. One night out is not worth fighting over during such a special and emotional time.

Casual

© photo by Barbie Hull Photography

- Play eighteen holes of golf and have a barbecue in the evening.

- Are you a video-game guy? Organize a Guitar Hero or Rock Band competition, or an old-school Atari or arcade game battle.

- Head to the hills for mountain biking in the summer or snowboarding in the winter.

- If you love to hunt, but it's not the right season, go to the firing range and learn to shoot a new gun, or play paintball with your guys.

218

Once his thoughts have been heard, talk about the guest list. Who are the most important people to invite? Will any family members be involved, like dads, brothers, or cousins? What will be appropriate activities for them?

The event planning should begin well in advance, and some things should be kept under wraps as a surprise for the groom. If the event requires travel, give everyone lots of time to make arrangements and be sensitive about budget restraints that may exclude some people from participating.

Themed

© photo by La Vie Photography

- For a Rat Pack or Swingers theme, hit a local casino, organize a poker tournament, or arrange a Scotch or whiskey tasting or a classic cocktail–mixing lesson at your favorite bar.

- Love the movie *The Big Lebowski?* Have a bowling tournament with your buddies and drink White Russians.

- Head to the racetrack and have everyone pitch in money for the groom to place his bets. Call ahead to see if you can get a private tour.

Weekend Destinations

© photo by Barbie Hull Photography

- Spend a weekend away at a local destination with your best buddies for some serious male bonding before the big day.

- Visit a city you've always wanted to see, like New York, Las Vegas, Chicago, or Austin, and meet up with your friends from around the country.

- A camping, hiking, or fishing trip provides lots of activities to keep you and your guys busy, as well as downtime for catching up and spending quality time together.

PARTIES & EVENTS

BACHELORETTE PARTY IDEAS

Play, party, and pamper yourself with a fun event that's just for the girls

During the busy time leading up to the wedding, time spent just with your girlfriends is a must for every bride-to-be. The bachelorette party can be organized by anyone close to the bride, and whether it's classic, casual, simple, or spectacular, it should be all about fun!

If the party will take place locally, schedule it at least two or three days before the wedding to allow for proper recovery time. Be sure to let out-of-town guests know the date so they can arrive in time to attend. If a destination weekend is more your style, plan way ahead and be sensitive about different people's budgets.

The bride is the guest at this party, so the host should

Classic

© photo by GH Kim Photography

- Now's your chance to get dressed up in your most fabulous fashions and hit the town!

- Treat the bride to a lovely dinner, and let her know how much she means to you. Be sure to reserve a table ahead of time.

- Let loose and go dancing. There's nothing but fun out on the dance floor with your girlfriends. Call around to find out where the bride's favorite kind of music will be played that night.

Casual

© photo by GH Kim Photography

- Whether it's a full day at the spa, or mini manis and pedis, a bachelorette party that involves pampering beauty treatments is a surefire winner.

- Take the bride to a karaoke bar and sing your heart out to your favorite tunes. Find

- out if the venue has private rooms if your girlfriends are on the shy side.

- Rent a hotel suite and have a sleepover. Order room service, have a dance party, and spend quality time catching up.

communicate with the rest of the group to organize payment in advance. Keep some of the events a surprise for added intrigue, and choose events and locations you know she'll love.

Gag gifts and racy toys are welcome at most bachelorette parties, and it's the perfect time to give her sexy lingerie and other fun items she may not have been comfortable opening at the bridal shower. Gifts at the bachelorette party can be far more casual or forgone for simply the gift of everyone's presence at the party.

Themed

© photo by GH Kim Photography

- Rent a boat and get the girls out on the water for an afternoon of lounging at sea.

- Host a wine tasting and invite an expert speaker to teach you all about wines from a region the bride loves. Chip in on a wine-of-the-month club gift for the newlyweds to enjoy.

- Take a fun hip-hop or swing-dance class, or invite a belly-dance instructor to the party to teach you all some new moves.

Weekend Destinations

© photo by Positive Light Photography

- Get out of town for an extended bachelorette party that includes both relaxation and excitement.

- Don't forget to bring any gag gifts, props, decorations, or presents along with you so you can get there and be relaxed and ready for fun.

- Choose a known party city, like Las Vegas, Miami, or New York, or a low-key destination she'll love.

- Camping, hiking, and playing sports aren't just for the guys. Get your girls together for a sporty weekend of outdoor fun.

PARTIES & EVENTS

EVENTS BEFORE & AFTER

Dinners, picnics, ball games, and brunches offer time to connect with family and friends

The days before and after your wedding are full of activity, and there are a few special events that will need planning.

Each wedding ceremony is unique, so it's important to schedule a rehearsal time to familiarize everyone involved with the specifics of yours. It will give you a great chance to see your planning come to life and make any final adjust-

ments to the timing, flow, and physical spacing of the ceremony. Check with the location coordinator so you know how much time you have there, and ask your maid of honor to keep an eye on the time so you're sure to cover everything.

After the rehearsal, the groom's parents traditionally host a dinner for the families, wedding party, and other important

Rehearsal

© photo by J. Garner Photography

- Schedule time a day or two before the wedding to practice your ceremony in your actual wedding location, and run through the program at least twice.

- Everyone involved in the ceremony should attend, including family and ushers.

- Bring a bouquet made of ribbon from your bridal shower gifts to hold as you walk down the aisle.

- Be sure all the guests involved know how to get to your ceremony location, since you may not have much time available there.

Rehearsal Dinner

© photo by GH Kim Photography

- At the rehearsal dinner the two of you should make a toast to your families, wedding party, and anyone else who has helped you along the way.

- For a more formal dinner, use a private room at your favorite restaurant or rent

- an event location and have a catered party.

- For a casual dinner, host a barbecue, picnic, or softball game in the park. It's a great way for family and guests to get to know each other.

out-of-town guests. A rehearsal dinner can be as casual as a backyard barbecue or as fancy as the wedding itself; it's totally up to you and the host. Try to make it an early night so you can all be well rested for the big day ahead.

Since you may not always have the opportunity to see the family and friends who are visiting for your wedding, organizing some group events is a great way for you to spend time relaxing and visiting with the ones you love. It's also a wonderful way for both of your families to get to know each other better if they're meeting for the first time.

The morning after your wedding, a leisurely brunch for everyone interested is a lovely way to wrap up the festivities and enjoy the company of your guests one last time. Say good-bye to travelers, chat with people you didn't get to see much the night before, and relive the high points of the wedding day.

Group Activities

© photo by J. Garner Photography

- Guests and family want to spend time with you, so even the simplest group events are meaningful.

- Buy a block of seats at a local professional baseball, basketball, football, or hockey game and invite your families and out-of-town guests to attend with you.

- Provide suggestions of fun events happening around town for visiting guests to enjoy in the days leading up to the wedding. Give them maps, directions, and information about where other guests are staying.

Postwedding Brunch

© photo by Barbie Hull Photography

- Schedule enough time so you can easily visit with your guests and say good-bye to out-of-town visitors, as well as eat a delicious breakfast.

- Reserve a private dining room at a location near where guests are staying,

or ask a family member to host it at his or her home.

- Help organize the event, but don't host brunch at your own house; you deserve to relax and rest the day after your wedding.

223

RESOURCES

The wedding world is full of amazing artists, talented professionals and inventive inspiration. This is by no means a complete list of wedding planning resources, but it will certainly help get you started. Use this list as a reference and a jumping off point, and look around in your own community for resources that will help you create the wedding you've been dreaming of.

Chapter 1: Wedding Style

Wedding Planning Articles, & Personal-Style Inspiration

Junebug Weddings
www.junebugweddings.com

Brides, Modern Bride & Elegant Bride magazines
www.brides.com

Grace Ormonde Wedding Style magazine
www.weddingstylemagazine.com

Inside Weddings magazine
www.insideweddings.com

InStyle Weddings magazine
www.instyleweddings.com

Martha Stewart Weddings
www.marthastewart.com/weddings

Pacific Weddings magazine
www.pacificweddings.com

Southern Weddings magazine
www.swsmag.net

Your Wedding Day magazine
www.yourweddingday.com

Chapter 2: Planning Basics

Wedding Planning Articles & Personal-Style Inspiration

Junebug Weddings
www.junebugweddings.com

Fun Tools, Toys & Communities

Color Palette Generator by Big Huge Labs
www.bighugelabs.com/flickr/colors.php

Indie Bride—forums for chatting with other brides-to-be
www.indiebride.com

Nearlyweds—personalized wedding Web sites
www.nearlyweds.com

The Wedding Report's Cost of Wedding Estimator
www.costofwedding.com

Green Wedding Resources

CarbonFund.org Zero Carbon Wedding Program
www.carbonfund.org/weddings

Earth Friendly Weddings
www.earthfriendlywedding.blogspot.com

Eco Chic Weddings
www.ecochicweddings.com

My Invitation Link
www.myinvitationlink.com

Portovert
www.portovert.com

Marriage License Requirements

U.S. Marriage Laws
www.usmarriagelaws.com

Wedding Blogs

What Junebug Loves
www.junebugweddings.com/blogs/what_junebug_loves

Blue Orchid Designs
www.blueorchidblog.com

The Bride's Café
www.thebridescafe.typepad.com

Brooklyn Bride
www.bklynbride.blogspot.com

From I Will to I Do
www.from-i-will-to-i-do.blogspot.com

Kiss the Groom
www.kissthegroom.com

Perfect Bound
www.perfectbound.blogspot.com

Ritzy Bee
www.ritzybee.typepad.com

Snippet and Ink
www.snippetandink.blogspot.com

Something Old, Something New
www.kenziekate.blogspot.com

Style Me Pretty
www.stylemepretty.com

Wedding Bee
www.weddingbee.com

Wedding Books

Carley Roney, *The Knot Complete Guide to Weddings in the Real World: The Ultimate Source of Ideas, Advice, and Relief for the Bride and Groom and Those Who Love Them*

Jung Lee, *Fête: The Wedding Experience*

Martha Stewart Living magazine, *The Best of Martha Stewart Living: Weddings*

Mindy Weiss and Lisbeth Levine, *The Wedding Book: The Big Book for Your Big Day*

Susie Coelho, *Style Your Dream Wedding*

Tara Guerard and Liz Banfield, *Southern Weddings: New Looks from the Old South*

Wedding Insurance

Protect My Wedding
www.protectmywedding.com

© photo by GH Kim Photography

Chapter 3: With This Ring

Diamond & Engagement Ring Information
Diamond Facts
www.diamondfacts.org

Interview with Emerson Robbins—five things to know when buying an engagement ring
www.junebugweddings.com
(Click on "Groombug," then "The Little Questions," then "Popping the Question")

The Kimberley Process
www.kimberleyprocess.com

Engagement & Wedding Rings—Alternative
Cathy Waterman
www.cathywaterman.com

Fancy
www.fancyjewels.com

Jamie Joseph
www.jamiejoseph.com

L. Frank
www.lfrankjewelry.com

Me & Ro
www.meandrojewelry.com

Reinstein/Ross
www.reinsteinross.com

Twist
www.twistonline.com

Engagement & Wedding Rings—Classic
Brilliant Earth
www.brilliantearth.com

Coast
www.coastdiamond.com

E.E. Robbins, the Engagement Ring Store
www.eerobbins.com

Gelin & Abaci
www.gelinabaci.com

Jeff Cooper
www.jeffcooperdesigns.com

Ritani
www.ritani.com

Tiffany and Co.
www.tiffany.com

Engagement & Wedding Rings—Vintage and Estate
Alana Antique and Estate Jewelry
www.alanajewelry.com

Antique and Estate Jewelry
www.antiqueandestate.com

Isadora's
www.isadoras.com

Men's Wedding Rings
Blue Nile
www.bluenile.com

Frederick Goldman
www.fgoldman.com

Lieberfarb
www.lieberfarb.com

Trent West
www.trewtungsten.com

Chapter 4: Choosing a Location

Wedding Planning Articles
& Personal-Style Inspiration
Junebug Weddings
www.junebugweddings.com

Destination Wedding Resources
Alison Events
www.alisonevents.com

Destination Weddings by the Knot
www.destinationweddingsbytheknot.com

Fly Away Weddings
www.flyawayweddings.com

Let's Run Off: Elopements Made Easy
www.letsrunoff.com

Luxe Destination Weddings
www.luxedestinationweddings.com

Tents & Coverings
Bella Umbrella
www.bellaumbrella.com

Raj Tents
www.rajtents.com

Chapter 5: Spread the Word

Wedding Planning Articles
& Personal-Style Inspiration
Junebug Weddings
www.junebugweddings.com

DIY Invitation Supplies
Blue Dot Paper Shop
www.bluedotpapershop.com

Kate's Paperie
www.katespaperie.com

Michael's
www.michaels.com

Moo Cards
www.moo.com

My Gatsby
www.mygatsby.com

Paper Source
www.paper-source.com

Paper Zone
www.paperzone.com

Wedding Invitations
Bella Figura
www.bellafigura.com

Elum
www.elumdesigns.com

Gryphon Stationers
www.gryphonstationers.com

Hello Lucky
www.hellolucky.com

227

Laura Hooper Calligraphy
www.lhcalligraphy.com

Minted
www.minted.com

Papeterie
www.papeteriestore.com

Wedding Paper Divas
www.weddingpaperdivas.com

Wiley Valentine
www.wileyvalentine.com

Chapter 6: Bride 101

Wedding Planning Articles & Personal-Style Inspiration

Junebug Weddings
www.junebugweddings.com

Customized Thank-You Notes & Stationery

Mimio
www.mimiopapers.com

Paper & Cup Design
www.papercupdesign.com

Simple Song Design
www.simplesongdesign.com

Simply Silhouettes
www.simplysilhouettes.com

Sugar Paper
www.sugarpaper.com

Etiquette Information

Emily Post
www.emilypost.com/weddings

Name Change Services

Miss Now Mrs.
www.missnowmrs.com

Name Birdie
www.namebirdie.com

Chapter 7: Groom 101

Men's Fashion Resources

Army dress uniform regulations
www.army.mil/history

Marines dress uniform regulations
www.marines.com

Navy dress uniform regulations
www.history.navy.mil

Shop Style Men
www.shopstyle.com/browse/mens-clothes

Style.com for men—GQ & Details magazines
www.men.style.com

Menswear Designers

Barneys New York
www.barneys.com

Brooks Brothers
www.brooksbrothers.com

Burberry
www.burberry.com

Calvin Klein
www.calvinklein.com

Hugo Boss
www.hugoboss.com

John Varvatos
www.johnvarvatos.com

Joseph Abboud
www.josephabboud.com

Men's Wearhouse
www.menswearhouse.com

Neiman Marcus
www.neimanmarcus.com

Nordstrom
www.nordstrom.com

Perry Ellis
www.perryellis.com

Ralph Lauren
www.ralphlauren.com

Web Sites for Grooms

Groom 411
www.groom411.com

Groom Groove
www.groomgroove.com

Junebug Weddings' Groombug
www.groombug.com

© photo by GH Kim Photography

Chapter 8: Health & Beauty

Beauty Inspiration, Information & Products

All About the Pretty blog
www.allaboutthepretty.typepad.com

Beauty Addict blog
www.beautyaddict.blogspot.com

Bella Sugar
www.bellasugar.com

Junebug Weddings' Fashion Report
www.junebugweddings.com

Makeup Bag blog
www.makeupbag.net

Sephora
www.sephora.com

Vogue magazine
www.style.com

Bridal Survival Kits

On the Go Kits
www.onthegokits.com

PHEW Kits
www.phewkits.com

Nutrition & Exercise Information

Fit Sugar
www.fitsugar.com

Shape magazine
www.shape.com

Women's Health magazine
www.womenshealthmag.com

Your Total Health
www.yourtotalhealth.ivillage.com

Chapter 9: Your Dress

Fashion Inspiration

Junebug Weddings' Fashion Report
www.junebugweddings.com

Style Bites
www.stylebites.blogspot.com

The Daily Obsession
www.thedailyobsession.net

The Sartorialist
www.thesartorialist.blogspot.com

Vogue magazine
www.style.com

Vintage & Consignment Wedding Dress Resources

Enokiworld
www.enokiworld.com

The Frock
www.thefrock.com

Once Wed
www.oncewed.com

Posh Girl Vintage
www.poshgirlvintage.com

Vintage Dress Pattern Resources

Grandma's House
www.grandmashouse.ws

Paper Pursuits
www.paperpursuits.com

The Vintage Pattern Lending Library
www.vpll.org

Wedding Dress & Accessory Designers

Amsale
www.amsale.com

Birnbaum and Bullock
www.birnbaumandbullock.com

Carolina Herrera
www.carolinaherrera.com

Claire Pettibone
www.clairepettibone.com

Elizabeth Fillmore
www.elizabethfillmorebridal.com

Jenny Packham
www.jennypackham.com

Kirstie Kelly Couture
www.kirstiekelly.com

Lela Rose
www.lelarose.com

Melissa Sweet
www.priscillaofboston.com

Monique Lhuillier
www.moniquelhuillier.com

Oscar de la Renta
www.oscardelarenta.com

Ramona Keveza
www.ramonakeveza.com

Reem Acra
www.reemacra.com

Vera Wang
www.verawangonweddings.com

Vineyard Collection
www.priscillaofboston.com

Chapter 10: Fashion

Jewelry

Abaloria
www.abaloria.com

Heidi Hull Designs
www.heidihulldesigns.com

Isadora's
www.isadoras.com

Jamie Joseph
www.jamiejoseph.com

Twist
www.twistonline.com

Lingerie

Agent Provocateur
www.agentprovocateur.com

Bare Necessities
www.barenecessities.com

Eberjey
www.eberjey.com

Elle Macpherson Intimates
www.ellemacphersonintimates.com

Figleaves
www.figleaves.com

Hanky Panky
www.hankypanky.com

Kiki de Montparnasse
www.kikidm.com

Mary Green
www.marygreen.com

Spanx
www.spanx.com

Shoes

Barneys New York
www.barneys.com

Bellissima Bridal Shoes
www.bellissimabridalshoes.com

Grace Footwear
www.gracefootwear.com

Net a Porter
www.net-a-porter.com

Shop Bop
www.shopbop.com

Vera Wang
www.verawangonweddings.com

Zappos
www.zappos.com

Veils, Hair Accessories & Fashion Extras

Bel Canto Designs
www.belcanto.etsy.com

Bella Umbrella
www.bellaumbrella.com

Erica Koesler
www.ericakoesler.com

Etsy
www.etsy.com

Jennifer Behr
www.jenniferbehr.com

Chapter 13: Photos & Video

A Hot List of Recommended Wedding Photographers & Videographers
Junebug Weddings
www.junebugweddings.com

Online Photo Sharing
Flickr
www.flickr.com

Smug Mug
www.smugmug.com

Snapfish
www.snapfish.com

Photo Albums — DIY
Blurb
www.blurb.com

Kolo Albums
www.koloalbums.com

My Publisher
www.mypublisher.com

Photo Albums — Handmade
Good Stock
www.good-stock.com

Jenni Bick
www.jennibick.com

Mary Adrene Designs
www.maryadrenedesigns.com

Photo Albums — Library Bound
Couture Book
www.couturebook.com

Graphi Studios
www.graphistudios.com

Kiss Wedding Books
www.kissweddingbooks.com

Leather Craftsman
www.leathercraftsman.com

Queensbury
www.queensbury.com

Chapter 14: Flowers

A Hot List of Recommended Florists
Junebug Weddings
www.junebugweddings.com

DIY Floral Options
DIY Bride
www.diybride.com

Floral Photo Inspiration
Junebug Weddings
www.junebugweddings.com

Brides, Modern Bride & Elegant Bride magazines
www.brides.com/weddingstyle/decorations

Flickr
www.flickr.com

Martha Stewart Weddings
www.marthastewart.com/weddings

Wedding Floral Design Books

Colin Cowie, *Colin Cowie Weddings*

Kimberly Aurora Kapur, *Bouquet Chic: Wedding Flowers for More Than 160 Romantic Looks*

David Stark and Avi Adler, *To Have and To Hold*

Chapter 15: Food & Cocktails

Amazing Cakes Shipped the World Over

Mike's Amazing Cakes
www.mikesamazingcakes.com

Cake & Cupcake Blogs

Cupcakes Take the Cake
www.cupcakestakethecake.blogspot.com

Pink Cake Box
www.blog.pinkcakebox.com

Chocolate, Candy, Cookies & Other Treats

Ali's Sweet Treats
www.alissweettreats.com

Beau-coup
www.beau-coup.com/cookie-wedding-party-favors.htm

Candy Favorites
www.candyfavorites.com

Candy Warehouse
www.candywarehouse.com

Fran's Chocolates
www.franschocolates.com

Gumdrop Cookie Shop
www.gumdropcookieshop.com

Groovy Candies
www.groovycandies.com

Ice Cream Source
www.icecreamsource.com

Theo Chocolate
www.theochocolate.com

The Well-Dressed Cookie
www.thewelldressedcookie.com

Cocktail & Drink Recipes

Drinksmixer
www.drinksmixer.com

The Modern Mixologist
www.themodernmixologist.com

Social Couture
www.socialcouture.typepad.com/tabletalk/drink_recipes

© photo by GH Kim Photography

Chapter 16: Entertainment

Dance Floor Rentals

Bickner Dance Floors
www.bicknerdancefloors.com

Dance Deck
www.dancedeck.com

Online Dance Lessons

Learn to Dance
www.learntodance.com

Chapter 17: The Ceremony

Cultural Wedding Traditions

Beau-coup
www.beau-coup.com/cultural-traditions-weddings.htm

World Wedding Traditions
www.worldweddingtraditions.com

Marriage License Requirements

Fly Away Weddings, destination requirements
www.flyawayweddings.com

U.K. Marriage Laws
www.wedding-services.demon.co.uk/marriage.htm

U.S. Marriage Laws
www.usmarriagelaws.com

Social Security Online
www.ssa.gov

Ordination Requirements

Be Ordained
www.beordained.com

Universal Life Church
www.theulc.com

Same-Sex Wedding Resources

Gay Weddings
www.gayweddings.com

Gay Weddings by the Knot
www.gayweddingsbytheknot.com

Wedding Vows

My Wedding Vows
www.myweddingvows.com

Chapter 18: Reception Details

Favors, Candles & Decor

Bliss Weddings Market
www.blissweddingsmarket.com

Estilo Weddings
www.estiloweddings.com

Glassy Baby
www.glassybaby.com

Ideal Favors
www.idealfavors.com

Ikea
www.ikea.com

Illuminations
www.illuminations.com

Plum Party
www.plumparty.com

Seating Charts
Simple Seating
www.simpleseating.com

Tenting & Linens
Raj Tents
www.rajtents.com

Wildflower Linen
www.wildflowerlinens.com

Wedding Decor Designers & Photo Galleries
Colin Cowie
www.colincowie.com

Details, Details
www.aboutdetailsdetails.com

Mary Dann
www.marydann.com

Michelle Rago
www.michelleragoltd.com

Mindy Weiss
www.mindyweiss.com

Oh, How Charming! by Lisa Vorce
www.ohhowcharming.com

Preston Bailey
www.prestonbailey.com

Rebecca Reategui
www.rebeccareategui.com

Chapter 19: Parties & Events
Food & Party Inspiration
Create My Event
www.createmyevent.com

Hostess with the Mostess
www.hwtm.com

Junebug Weddings' Groombug
www.groombug.com

Matthew Mead
www.matthewmeadstyle.com

Yum Sugar
www.yumsugar.com

Party Supplies, Favors & Decor
Estilo Weddings
www.estiloweddings.com

Mini Word Magnets
www.miniwordmagnets.com

Plum Party
www.plumparty.com

Weddingish
www.weddingish.com

ACKNOWLEDGMENTS

Thank you!

At Junebug Weddings we're passionate about working in a collaborative environment in order to benefit, support, and encourage everyone involved in our business and our community. The creation of this book was the ultimate collaborative process, and it would not have been possible without our friends, our families, and the generous support of the professional wedding community. Below are the names of the people who contributed to this book and supported our vision. We owe them all a great big THANK YOU for sharing their talents, artistry, and energy with us! They have our eternal gratitude and admiration.

Thank you to the stunningly talented photographers whose artistry brings this book to life. Look for their photo credits listed on each page.
  GH Kim Photography: www.ghkim.com
  John and Joseph Photography: www.jkhphoto.com
  One Thousand Words Photography:
      www.onethousandwordsphotography.com
  Barbie Hull Photography: www.barbiehull.com
  Jenny Jimenez Photography: www.photojj.com
  J. Garner Photography: www.jgarnerphoto.com
  Cheri Pearl Photography: www.cheripearl.com
  Yours by John Photography: www.yoursbyjohn.com
  La Vie Photography: www.laviephoto.com
  Positive Light Photography: www.positivelightphotography.com

Thank you to the models whose faces grace these pages:
  Vivian Hsu
  Amanda Wall
  Alyssa Cave
  Leah Ferrel

Thank you to the bridal salon owners and dress designers for sharing their style:
  The Bridal Garden: www.thebridalgarden.com
  Lea-Ann Belter: www.lea-annbelter.com
  Birnbaum & Bullock: www.birnbaumandbullock.com
  Judd Waddell: www.juddwaddell.com
  La Belle Reve: www.labellereve.com
  Manuel Mota for Pronovias: www.pronovias.com
  Erica Koesler: www.ericakoesler.com
  Heidi Hull Designs: www.heidihulldesigns.com
  Ann Marie Lingerie
  Simone Perel
  Jonquil: www.jonquillingerie.com
  Sherry et Cie: www.sherryetcie.com
  Huit: www.huit.fr
  Isadora's: www.isadoras.com
  Madina Vadache: www.madinavadache.com
  Luly Yang Couture: www.lulyyang.com

Thank you to the cake designers who make our mouths water:
  New Renaissance Cakes: www.newrenaissancecakes.com
  Jen's Desserts: www.jensdesserts.com
  Lisa Dupar Catering: www.lisaduparcatering.com
  Crème de la Crème: www.cakesbycremedelacreme.com
  Mike's Amazing Cakes: www.mikesamazingcakes.com
  Trophy Cupcakes: www.trophycupcakes.com
  Tallant House: www.tallanthouse.com
  B&O Espresso

Thank you to the florists whose passion for beauty enriches us all:
  Juniper Flowers: www.juniperflowers.com
  Bella Rugosa: www.bellarugosa.com
  Acanthus Floral: www.acanthusfloral.com
  Christopher Flowers: www.christopherflowers.biz

ACKNOWLEDGMENTS

Woodland Flowers: www.woodlandflowers.com
Fiore Blossoms: www.fioreblossoms.com
Aria Style: www.ariastyle.com
Garden Party Floral: www.gardenpartyflowers.com
Loves Me Flowers: www.lovesmeflowers.com
Athena Flora: www.athenaflora.com
Laurie Cinotto: www.lauriecinotto.com

Thank you to the invitation designers who know how to tell it:
  Brown Sugar Design: www.bsdstudio.com
  All About Weddings: www.allaboutweddingsnw.com
  Bella Figura: www.bellafigura.com
  Ephemera Custom Letterpress: www.ephemera-press.com
  Izzy Girl: www.izzygirl.com
  Paper Moxie: www.papermoxie.com
  Mmm Paper: www.mmmpaper.com
  A and O Design: www.aandodesign.com

Thank you to the jewelers who bring the sparkle and shine:
  E.E. Robbins, the Engagement Ring Store: www.eerobbins.com
  Ritani: www.ritani.com
  Gelin & Abaci: www.gelinabaci.com
  Jeff Cooper: www.jeffcooperdesigns.com
  Coast: www.coastdiamond.com
  Lieberfarb: www.lieberfarb.com
  Frederick Goldman: www.fgoldman.com
  Trent West: www.trewtungsten.com
  Twist: www.twistonline.com
  Jamie Joseph: www.jamiejoseph.com
  Me & Ro: www.meandrojewelry.com
  Reinstein/Ross: www.reinsteinross.com
  L. Frank: www.lfrankjewelry.com
  Marie-Helene de Taillac: www.mariehelenedetaillac.com
  Taru
  Fancy: www.fancyjewels.com

Greenlake Jewelry Works: www.greenlakejewelryworks.com
Isadora's: www.isadoras.com

Thank you to the event professionals who provide products and expertise that exceed expectations:
  Good Taste Events: www.goodtasteevents.com
  PHEW Kits: www.phewkits.com
  Totally Tabletops: www.totallytabletops.com
  Clara French Ceramics: www.clarafrench.com
  Tolo Events: www.toloevents.com
  Pedersen's Event Rentals: www.pedersens.com
  Rented Elegance: www.rentedelegance.com
  Grand Event Rentals: www.grandeventrentals.com
  Mosaic Linens: www.partymosaic.com

Thank you to Erin Skipley of Bellatrix Studio, whose way with hair and makeup makes getting gorgeous easy: www.bellatrixstudio.com.

Thank you to Pravda Studios for providing a fun, hip place to take commercial photos in Seattle: www.pravdastudios.com.

Last but definitely not least, THANK YOU to our friends and family for their love, patience, and support: Adam Bamberg, Ron and Kandace Loewen, Bob and Reid deLaubenfels, Sydnor Hain, Chela Weber, Karen Scott, Sylvia Moore, Mike Weber and Fran Vasconcellos, Matt Hemeyer, Mike Stancliff, Katy Browning, Jeff Hopkins, and Tracey Peyton.

Thank you, thank you, thank you, from the bottom of our hearts.

xoxo,
Blair, Kim, and Christy

INDEX